TOTAL JUSTICE

Also available in the
Russell Sage Foundation
75th Anniversary Series

Notes on Social Measurement
Historical and Critical
by Otis Dudley Duncan

Big Structures
Large Processes
Huge Comparisons
by Charles Tilly

TOTAL JUSTICE

Lawrence M. Friedman

RUSSELL SAGE FOUNDATION   NEW YORK

The Russell Sage Foundation

Library of Congress Cataloging-in-Publication Data

Friedman, Lawrence Meir, 1930–
    Total justice / Lawrence M. Friedman.
        p.   cm.
    Includes bibliographic references and index.
    ISBN: 0-87154-297-8
    ISBN: 0-87154-268-4 (pbk)
    1. Justice, Administration of—United States.   2. Sociological
jurisprudence.   I. Title.
KF384.F75 1985
340.115—dc19   84-51638
                                                                   CIP

First paperback edition 1994

Preface to the paperback edition
© 1994 by Russell Sage Foundation

RUSSELL SAGE FOUNDATION
112 East 64th Street, New York, New York 10021

10 9

to LEAH, JANE, AMY, and SARAH

PREFACE

Total Justice was an attempt to explore and explain American legal culture. When I wrote this short book, the air was filled with shouts and complaints about how litigious we were in the United States. The same shouts and complaints can still be heard. I was then and am today skeptical about these claims. To be sure, law, lawyers, and legal institutions are central to American life. But I saw little hard evidence that people in this country were "litigious," in the sense of some sort of habit or addiction. Nonetheless, Americans do seem rights-conscious, on the whole; and American legal culture, in the contemporary period, has certain distinctive features that seem worthy of exploration. My aim in 1985 was not to praise or blame anybody; but to bore a hole into the core of our legal system and examine it as objectively as I could. What I found, or thought I found, made up the body of this book.

The basic idea concerned a shift in legal culture—corresponding to a shift in general social norms—toward a culture of redress through law that I called the urge for "total justice." I tried to connect this urge with certain brute facts concerning the modern state and the social revolution that technology brought about. I became convinced that the trend toward "total justice," as I saw it, was in fact common to the whole Western world. It was not distinctively American, although perhaps it took a somewhat extreme form in the United States.

Everything in the book depended on the simple but essential assumption that a living legal order is not "autonomous," or self-contained. Rather, it is organic to whatever society it is located in, and it draws its vital juices from that society. Of course, some systems are better or more just than others; some are corrupt and inefficient, others less so. To *understand* a legal system, and what makes it tick, is not to excuse its shortcomings or to be complacent about the way it operates and what it does to people. But, in my view, unless we try to understand the social roots of the way things are, there is little hope of meaningful reform. I did not want my book to be thought of as right-wing or left-wing or any-wing, but as an honest search for the meaning of historical trends and events. Some people would consider such an aim naive or misguided. I do not.

Since I wrote this book, nothing has changed in any *essential* regard. As I see it, the urge for total justice is a massive, powerful global force; and there are no signs that it can or will abate. Each generation defines freedom, liberty, the good life, in its own inimitable way. Total justice is one aspect of modern culture: most people are not aware of it on a conscious level. But it is a vital part of the actions and thoughts of countless men and women who use or aspire to use law. I hope this book has added, in some small way, to our understanding of the living legal order—or at least to the quality of the debate.

LAWRENCE M. FRIEDMAN

Stanford, California
March 1994

CONTENTS

PART I   1

Chapter 1.   The Problem Stated   3
Chapter 2.   The Law: Creatures from Inner Space   6
Chapter 3.   The Birth of a Modern Legal Culture   38
Chapter 4.   The Security State   45
Chapter 5.   The Due Process Revolution   80

PART II   95

Chapter 6.   American Legal Character   97
Chapter 7.   Sexual Behavior and the Law: A Case in Point   126
Chapter 8.   An Assessment   147
Chapter 9.   Epilogue: A Note on the Wide, Wide World   153

Acknowledgments   157

Index   159

PART I

1

THE PROBLEM STATED

ONE OF THE MOST striking aspects of American society, to natives and foreigners alike, is the way law and the legal system seem to dominate public life—and, apparently, much private life as well. There are, as we shall see, an extraordinary number of lawyers in this country; and they seem to be multiplying like rabbits. In general, law appears to be growing at an alarming pace. If an outside observer took the daily newspaper as a rough guide to events and situations that worry or excite Americans, he would conclude that sports and law are the two main topics of interest in the country. And law has even been creeping into the sports pages, with stories about contracts for basketball players, court struggles over team franchises, and so on. Any reader can make the test for herself, picking up at random any copy of any newspaper, any day. Almost every domestic story has a legal angle. Almost every story mentions a judge, a court, a rule, the police, the state legislature, Congress, some administrative agency, somebody suing somebody— *some* aspect of law, some rule or regulation.

This emphasis on legal process—this obsession with law—strikes many observers as unique to the United States, an impression that is reinforced by newspaper and magazine articles that talk about the "law explosion." There is also the impression that the "explosion" began rather recently and is getting worse as time goes on. By common agreement, too, the law explosion is something to worry about. The feeling is that there is a runaway legal system in this country, a system out of control.

This short book is written in the hope of shedding some light on the problem, if there is a problem. I will discuss some aspects of the modern legal system—aspects which, I believe, help account for its amazing growth. If we understand better where the legal system comes from, we may come to understand where it might be going, or at least what it is doing now.

Every country in the world has its own legal system, but this book is primarily about the United States. From time to time I will refer to other countries. My argument rests on evidence drawn mostly from American experience, but it is also a general argument about modern societies, and if it has nothing to say about other Western countries, then it is probably wrong. (A brief epilogue discusses the cross-cultural question.)

The first chapter outlines the problem, as critics of the system tend to see it. At the most general level, the subject is a cluster of trends in American law that arouse a widespread sense of crisis or unease. The argument compares legal institutions and processes as they are today with the way they were in in the past. Hence, this is a book about *changes* in the legal system, changes that have taken place mostly in the past hundred years or so. The problem of change in the legal system is of course not a "problem" in the usual sense—that is, it is not some sort of difficulty that has to be solved; it is a problem only in the intellectual sense. But exploration of this historical problem should illuminate modern conditions and the current sense of crisis.

Compared to a century ago, there is more of just about every aspect of our legal system —more lawyers, more cases, more statutes, more rules and regulations. To the jaundiced eyes of some observers, the lawyers are running the country, a condition they consider totally deplorable. There is a great wringing of hands, a great chorus of complaints, all up and down the land. One writer asks whether "lawyering" is not about to "strangle democratic capitalism."[1] Others see lawyers not as enemies of the status quo, but as hyperactive protectors of the establishment. In any event, the legal system can often seem completely out of bounds.

The central theme of this book can be simply stated. There is, in actual fact, a kind of "law explosion" in this country. That is, there has been, over the last century or so, a tremendous increase in certain uses of legal process. It is, on the other hand, misleading or downright wrong to think of this as a *litigation* explosion. Courts have not expanded their work quantitatively as much as the work has altered in a more qualitative sense.

The American legal system has undergone tremendous change in the last century or so. But it is not right to focus too much attention on courts, litigation, and lawyers. These legal actors and institutions merely reflect what is happening in society as a whole. There have been, in the period mentioned, enormous changes in social organization, which in turn have had an impact on legal culture—on the level of demands that people make on the legal system. How all this works to transform the law, and what the changes mean to American society, is the theme of this book.

There are many of these changes, and they are complex and interwoven. But they seem to be moving in certain definite directions. There has developed in this country what I call here a *general expectation of justice*, and a *general expectation of recompense for injuries and loss*. Together, these make up a demand for what will be called "total justice." A demand, of course, is not a response. But the argument here is that the legal system has taken a number of significant steps toward fulfilling these demands—not without protest, not without countermovement, of course; but toward total justice nonetheless. This, in short, is the story.

NOTES

1. Laurence H. Silberman, "Will Lawyering Strangle Democratic Capitalism?" *Regulation* 2 (1978): 15.

2

THE LAW: CREATURES FROM INNER SPACE

IN A CHEAP HORROR MOVIE that was popular a while back, the world was invaded by some sort of living goo from outer space that spread relentlessly, gobbling up absolutely everything in its path. Some of the cries of alarm about the American legal system picture law as a phenomenon very much like this blob from outer space, growing relentlessly and swallowing up billions of dollars and whole social institutions as it spreads. Everybody, it is said, is suing everybody else. There is a serious "litigation explosion." The machinery of law is breaking down. There is a "crisis" on our hands. What the crisis consists of, and why it is a crisis, is never made entirely clear; but that there is a crisis—of legitimacy, and in the operating system—is a point on which scholars tend to agree, right, left, and center.

The point also has international backing. In fact, European intellectuals are among the main purveyors of the "crisis" idea, the notion that Western governments and their legal systems face a dreadful turning point. They have packaged various versions of the problem under a number of names, including the "legitimation crisis," a dreadful state of affairs that seriously threatens "system integration."[1] Whatever system integration may mean, it is clearly bad medicine to threaten it. There are also complaints that the modern state has become "ungovernable"; that the problems of contemporary life have outstripped the capacity of governmental organs to control them, or to solve the problems.[2] Complaints are also heard in Europe about the "flood of norms," which match the complaints in this country about the "law explosion."[3]

On what are these fearful images based, and should they be taken seriously? The problem of the general system crisis—the crisis, if any, of integration and social stability that endangers the Western world—is beyond the scope of this book. It is mentioned here only because it is related, conceptually and psychologically, to the notion of a crisis in the legal system; this is in turn related to the idea of a law explosion, that is, an elephantiasis of the legal system, which struggles to do work it is not equipped to do. Is there a law explosion? If there is, what has caused it, and is it harmful to our social health? If there is not, or if the explosion is not the same as pictured, then what is giving off the false impressions? Where there is smoke, there is usually fire.

Criticism of the American legal system tends to focus on three types of excess. There are too many lawyers, too much law, and too much litigation. Each of these charges will be examined in turn. I will then go on to an alternative view of the modern legal system, described in historical and social terms.

Too Many Lawyers

On this point everyone seems to agree: the sheer size of the profession has gotten out of hand. This sentiment is to be expected from the man and woman on the street; but it is also heard in high places. The president of Harvard University, Derek Bok, a lawyer himself (and former dean of the Harvard Law School), made a major speech in April 1983, in which he proceeded, methodically and deliberately, to bite the hand that once fed him. He talked about the sins of the

American legal system as a whole ("among the most expensive and least efficient in the world"); but he also complained bitterly about the legal profession. Too many "able" college graduates were going to law school. This meant a "massive diversion of exceptional talent" into "pursuits" that were, frankly, parasitic. Lawyers and lawsuits produce nothing; not nuts and bolts, not bread or sausages, not works of art, not "culture or the enhancement of the human spirit." The lawyers instead strew the scene with social wreckage: conflict, complexity, and confusion.

No question: the legal profession is very big and getting bigger, and the pace of growth is getting faster and faster. In the spring of 1984, something on the order of 650,000 men and women were practicing law in this country. This means there was about 1 lawyer for every 350 people living in the United States.

But a bloated legal profession is an old fact of life in the United States. Lawyers were a scarce commodity during the colonial period, but their numbers began to increase after the Revolution, and they have been leaping ahead ever since. In 1740, there were only 15 lawyers in the colony of Massachusetts Bay, serving a population of about 150,000. In 1840, a hundred years later, there were 640 lawyers in the state of Massachusetts, ten times as many in proportion to the population.[4]

That was only the start. Sometime before 1900, the profession passed the 100,000 mark. In 1950, there were about 200,000 lawyers, roughly 1 for every 750 Americans.[5] Between 1960 and 1970, the numbers increased by about a third; and between 1970 and 1975, new admissions to the bar went up by an amazing 91 percent.[6] There are currently about 40,000 new lawyers hatched every year. At this rate, unless something happens to save the nation, at some point in the distant future every living soul in the country will be a member of the bar.

That paradise is a long way off, but it is certainly no surprise that a lot of people wonder what all these lawyers (especially the new ones) are up to, what work and what mischief they do, and whether the country really needs all of these lawyers. Not everybody who graduates law school finds a law job, of course. Some become claims adjusters, or bank tellers. Some go into business. Some will have to sell real estate or shoes. But the country cannot bank on solving the "problem" of excess lawyers through attrition. An enormous corps of lawyers is part of the national heritage, and part of the future, as far as the eye can see.

Of course, the sheer number of lawyers does not mean much in itself. There is no obvious measuring rod for deciding whether there are too many or too few lawyers in the country. It is interesting, though, to look at the experience of other countries. The United States *appears* to be way out in front in terms of making and using lawyers. It is the Saudi Arabia of lawyers, the leading world producer, dominant here as it is in coal, jumbo jets, and types of salamander. Other modern countries make do with a much lower number of lawyers per thousand population. This is true of France, Italy, and Holland— even the motherland of the common law, Great Britain.

The most startling example is Japan. The population is about half that of the United States, so that we would expect about half as many lawyers, something on the order of 300,000. In fact they have less than a tenth the expected amount. Yet Japan has a gigantic, successful economy, and does brilliantly on the world market. It seems obvious that lawyers are doing something for us or to us that the Japanese are doing without; or perhaps there is some other occupational group in Japan that does what lawyers do here. Who or what that might be must remain unsettled.

Actually, things are never quite what they seem. One might imagine that a lawyer is a lawyer is a lawyer; in fact there are serious problems in measuring and comparing legal professions across cultures.[7] Still, there is no question that the United States has many lawyers. That there are too many requires, of course, a further argument. After all, nobody would argue that there are too many houses, or pencils, or carpenters; most of us assume some rough balance between supply and demand. If people buy a lot of ice cream, it is because they want a lot; if they hire a lot of landscape architects, it is because they feel a need for their services. Why is the case of lawyers different? Why reject the idea that the supply is a response to a big demand?

The critics make, essentially, two points: first, that lawyers create demand, which means that the demand is at least partly artificial. If there are too many lawyers, it is hard for them to make an honest living; hungry lawyers think up legalisms, foment litigation, and make trouble. Almost everybody "knows" a situation where this happened. The literature also mentions "meter-running," that is, ways in which lawyers spend useless time, building up billable hours they can stick (rich) clients with.[8]

There is no reason to be totally skeptical. Nobody ever claimed that all lawyers were honest and selfless; quite the contrary. Lawyers also have gained a monopoly on many activities, not all of which really need to be done by lawyers. Thus the professional activities of lawyers do keep the demand for lawyers artificially high. But this is not the same as creating the demand for what lawyers do.

On the other hand, it is hard to find evidence for any large-scale aggregate effect of lawyer-work (or make-work) on the demand for legal services. Even the evidence of "meter-running" is not easy to assess. Huge corporations are, indeed, willing to spend a lot of money on legal services, and they know that their kind of lawyer comes with a high price tag. My own inclination is to accept the general idea that demand here pushes supply. Yes, as Derek Bok bemoaned, very able minds *are* attracted to law; but this may be precisely because of the enormous demand for lawyers' services—demands that in the ultimate measure they did not create by themselves. In a way, the bulk of this book will be devoted to exploring where this demand comes from and why.

The second argument raised against lawyers is that they are much too powerful. They dominate the legislatures, they run the government, they shape the policies of administrative agencies and private corporations. There is no doubt that lawyers occupy political jobs out of all proportion to their number, and have done so since the dawn of the Republic; but it is not clear what difference this makes to legislative output.[9] The influence of lawyers on business behavior is also problematic.[10] Perhaps the heart of the complaint is that all this lawyering (Bok's point again) is a sign of a sick, conflict-ridden society, a society riddled with waste and eaten away by parasites. This may or may not be true, but the problem (if there is one) is less a matter of lawyers than of law. This brings us to number two of the three general complaints: too many laws.

Too Many Laws

Of the making of books, said Ecclesiastes, there is no end; one might perhaps say the same about law.

It is almost certainly true that there is more sheer legal *stuff* today than there was a century ago. But there is a difficult problem of measurement, which must be confronted at the outset. What is a law, or a "rule," and how can we count these? Nobody has yet come up with a satisfactory answer.

One could, of course, go through the statute books (federal and state) and count pages; one could count numbers of new statutes, or try to analyze and count the many separate rules or propositions inside the texts of these statutes. It is not clear what one would have when the job was finished; at any rate, nobody has done this, and considering what a boring, thankless job it would be, nobody is likely to.

The problems get even worse if one tries to get some notion of the sheer size of the whole law, including rules which are not part of statutory codes. Which of these should be taken into account? The rules of administrative agencies? City ordinances? The operating rules of the Port of New York Authority, which runs bridges, terminals, and bus stations? The rules of the New Orleans school board? And what shall be done with that body of rules that, in a way, most typifies the common law: doctrines contrived by the courts that form the premises of reasoning in decided cases? Catching and counting these is like catching and counting the wind.

In short, measuring the number of "laws," or the size of the corpus of law, is a pretty hopeless task. But there is little question about the fact of growth. Take statutes (enacted laws), for example. In the first part of the nineteenth century, in the typical American state, the whole body of statute laws fit neatly into a single volume or two. The Revised Statutes of Ohio, as of 1841, consisted of one fat book of 1,003 pages. This is nothing compared to the modern Revised Statutes of Ohio and other states, which typically fill a whole shelf. The statutes are puffed up, it is true, with "annotations," but then these too are part of the law. The pace of statutory growth seems to be accelerating. More and more statutes are proposed, debated, and passed. In 1975, for example, 4,331 bills were introduced into the two houses of California's legislature.[11]

The growth of administrative rules is even more striking. On the federal level, in the nineteenth century, agencies generated a mere handful of new norms each year—tariff rules; rules about excise taxes; rules about the public lands. The growth of federal administrative regulation in the last generation has been nothing short of spectacular. Since the late 1930s, new rules and regulations, executive orders, and the like, have been reported in the Federal Register. The first full year of the Register was 1937, and that year it ran to 3,450 pages. By 1963 it had reached 14,842 pages; the total for 1980 was an astonishing 87,012 pages; in 1981 it dropped to a mere 58,494. This is still a colossal output of legal matter.

There has been striking growth as well in rules and regulations on the local level—state administrative agencies, of which there are dozens in the typical state; rules put out by cities and towns; and rules of such local agencies as school boards and sewer districts. Land-use planning rules—zoning is a major example—virtually did not exist until the 1920s. Today, they are a great legal enterprise.

There has also been, very notably, a tremendous surge of rules and rule making in private institutions. Of course, the rules of a hospital, a (private) university, or a business concern are not "law" in the sense of "governmental social control," which is the way Donald Black defines law.[12] But they are an important phenomenon in their own right. And very often (though not always) these rules come about in response to government action, to what is clearly "governmental social control"; in other words, in response to "legal" rules. General Motors no doubt has an elaborate inner structure of rules about employees—hiring policies, overtime pay, safety on the job, and retirement and pensions. Government programs, rules, provisions form the background for most of these internal rules. "The law" does not explain *all* the private rules of this gigantic company, but it is a significant element.

People refer to the "judicialization" or "legalization" of private institutions, and these terms do seem apt. What all this means exactly is an issue that will be taken up later, in more detail. A simple example will do for now. Around 1900, there were no formal, written rules in the little red schoolhouse about what children were supposed to wear and how they were supposed to behave in school. The teacher had authority to run the classroom, and there were no procedures for testing the limits of the teacher's authority, except in the rarest of cases.

All this, of course, has changed dramatically in the last generation or so. There were, for example, about seventy-five federal cases in the late 1960s and early 1970s on an issue the nineteenth century would have found totally inconceivable: rules about the way high-school boys wore their hair. Many of these cases about hair length, sideburns, mustaches, and beards were appealed to the Circuit Court level and were taken very seriously.[13] There are also by now hundreds of school cases about desegregation, rights of handicapped children, sex discrimination, bilingual education, and the like. "Law and education" had become for the first time a "field" of law.

Credit or blame for these developments cannot be laid entirely at the door of the courts. Courts, to be sure, have spun new webs of doctrine. But there is also a great deal of new legislation that affects the way schools are run. The courts did not create the programs for handicapped children, for example, that have generated a whole host of new rules.[14] And, of course, legislation and court cases reflect what is happening inside as well as outside the school systems. Internally, the schools have been "legalized" or, if you will, bureaucratized. The little red schoolhouse is no more, and little-red-schoolhouse-style law has gone with it.

The discussion so far has referred mainly to rules and regulations, both public and private. Law, however, is not merely rules and regulations that are imposed by government on passive subjects. The legal system is, first of all, a system of interactions or processes, both internal and external. The "subjects" outside the system interact with the people inside. I will use two convenient phrases to describe a bit more precisely those activities and behaviors inside society that concern law and the legal system: *legal act* and *legal behavior*.

I use the term *legal act* to refer to relevant behavior by people with authority who act inside the legal system.[15] A new statute passed in North Dakota is a legal act; so, quite obviously, is any decision handed down by a judge or an administrator. Laws and rules and regulations are only a small part of the total number of legal acts that are performed in society every day. Every time a police officer stops traffic, or issues a ticket, or arrests a burglar, he or she has committed a legal act. The same is true every time a clerk in city hall issues a marriage, dog, or hunting license. The total number of legal acts is therefore impossible to measure. But it seems obvious that there must be many more today than even a generation ago. The number of (potential) legal actors is after all very great. Millions are on public payrolls. Big legal acts (major statutes or decisions) breed middle-sized legal acts (rules and regulations by agencies), which in turn generate dozens of small legal acts (the behavior of officials, police officers, and civil servants).

There has no doubt also been an enormous increase in *legal behavior* which I define as any direct or indirect response to a legal act.[16] When a person consciously "obeys" a law, this is legal behavior, as is deliberate disobedience or evasion. In the broadest sense, there is a good deal of legal behavior that is neither obedience nor disobedience; rather, it is behavior influenced by some legal act, or by awareness of some rule or law, or by the presence of a legal actor. If I choose Highway 280 over Highway 101 because I think there is less chance that the police are cruising on 280; if I switch from hunting wolves to hunting rabbits because it is illegal to hunt wolves, these are examples of legal behavior.

Obviously, it is impossible to measure legal behavior as a whole, just as it is impossible to measure legal acts in the aggregate. But it seems clear that the amount of legal behavior in society must also be increasing. Legal behavior is behavior in response to legal acts; if there are more legal acts, there will be more legal behavior.

Just as we wondered whether the large number of lawyers means something is amiss in society, so too can we ask whether something is radically wrong with a society so profuse with legal acts and legal behavior. But there is no baseline or standard of measurement, and there is no way to compare societies, at least not societies that are contemporary with each other. Many people think that Americans litigate more than the French do, and there are certainly more lawyers here per thousand population. But because legal acts and legal behaviors cannot be quantified, no one can effectively make the case that there are more of them in the United States than there are in France.

Of course, France might also be in desperate shape. But, in truth, it is impossible to say how much legal behavior is too much. Not only is there no adequate measure, there is no agreed-on standard of conduct for people and societies we can use to measure against. Certainly, many people think we have too much law, too much legal behavior, and that something should be done about it. The president of Harvard says so; he echoes, in somewhat more elegant tones, voices heard in the press, in the magazines, on television. The critics tell horror stories and recount anecdotes, but they are remarkably short on facts and figures. They are skimpy on notions of cause and effect. And they fail to tell us why legal behavior is so noxious. It is certainly not self-evident that a society that pays a great deal of attention to rules of law is sick or conflicted beyond repair.

The question is: why is there so much law? Is it doing more harm than good? The answers are not obvious, and it may well be that there are no general answers. For now, one point should be made: if there is a tremendous supply of some commodity in our society, it can be explained in two general ways. The first is the concept of supply and demand. We produce a lot of chickens because we eat a lot of chickens. The market adjusts supply and demand. The second explanation is that something is distorting the market. Because of price supports, for example, we may have mountains of unwanted cheese. Because of something in the structure of society, or in institutional forms, there might be an overproduction of laws.[17] My own general bias is that the supply of law in modern America is more like the chicken than the cheese. Later this book will explore some sources of the "explosion" of legal acts. Meanwhile let us proceed to the third of our "too many's," the alleged explosion of litigation.

Too Many Lawsuits: The Litigation Explosion

If there is one thing the public and, to a large extent, the legal profession itself seems sure of, it is that we are in the midst of a "litigation explosion." There seems to be a deluge of lawsuits, overwhelming society and its courts. But it is not easy to tell whether or not this is true. In principle, litigation (actual cases) should be much easier to quantify than laws, legal acts, or legal behavior; in practice, as we will see, there are serious gaps in the evidence, and serious problems of measurement. There is reason to doubt whether the litigation explosion is as real as most people seem to think it is; in any event, the subject has to be approached more cautiously than it has been in the popular press or even the scholarly literature.[18]

There are indeed constant complaints that the country is suffering from a terrible case of too much suing. Judges warn the public that the system is so jammed with cases that the whole creaky structure is about to tumble down. We read items in newspapers and magazines about the "suing society." As one article put it, "Everybody is suing everybody"; this is an "age of litigation."[19] One writer coined the rather hysterical term "hyperlexis" to describe this "national disease"; it has, he said, "overloaded" the circuits of the law.[20] Even those who should know better sometimes get swept up in the tide; Jethro K. Lieberman's book on the American litigation system, though it deals with the issue quite sensibly, carries the unfortunate title *The Litigious Society*.[21]

The consequences of "hyperlexis" seem clear, at least to the people who complain most loudly. First, the court system itself is bound to collapse. Justice delayed is justice denied, and more and more delay is bound to come. Second, all this suing impairs the legitimate business of government. Running the country is hard enough in the best of times; it becomes totally impossible if every Tom, Dick, and Mary can rush into court to check, obstruct, or reverse any public action they disapprove of. Third, there is damage to the very fabric of our society. Litigation drives up prices, adds to the tax burden, and inflates the cost of insurance. Business is forced to spend vast amounts of money on lawyers and legal defense. Worst of all is the effect on the quality of life. To quote a popular news magazine, "as employees sue employers, students sue teachers, taxpayers sue bureaucrats and friends sue friends, trust is undermined and creativity discouraged."[22]

Curiously enough, the people who make these charges do not back them up with precise, hard evidence. There is a vast literature of invective, but most of it is devoid of quantitative measures and empirical findings. The few actual numbers usually relate to *federal* litigation. Federal litigation *has* been rising faster than the population,[23] and this is a significant fact. But in the American system, there are state courts as well as federal courts, and 95 percent or more of the cases filed, dealt with, and disposed of, begin and end in state and local courts, not federal courts. State court cases may number in the millions. What do we know about the work of state courts, and, in particular, about the volume of cases over time?

Surprisingly little. State courts are understudied, and their work, until recently, has been badly measured.[24] But before one can even discuss the state courts and their work, there is a threshold question: Exactly what is meant by a "litigation explosion"? What would such an explosion look like, and how would we know one if we saw one?

The answer is far from clear. Presumably, a litigation explosion means a rapid, powerful increase in litigation rates. A litigation "rate" must refer to some relationship between the size of the population and the amount of litigation—an index, say, of the number of court cases filed or decided each year per thousand population. No such figure is available in a convenient, accurate time-series, and even if it were, it is not clear how it should be interpreted. There is no standard for deciding how much litigation is a lot or a little. The implication is that there is a lot today, much more than yesterday and the day before yesterday, and that there is a great deal more in the United States than in other countries. This means, then, that there should be some way to compare litigation rates today with the rates in the past, and some way to compare American litigation rates with those of other countries.

But the comparative evidence is murky and inconclusive.[25] And historical comparisons are hard to work with. First of all, there are no neat historical figures, gathered by a Census Bureau or other helpful agency. There is no aggregate data at all for the nineteenth and much of the twentieth centuries. Studies are needed comparing the flow of work through courts in different time periods. But there are only a handful of such studies, none of them totally satisfactory, drawn from a melange of places—Chippewa County, Wisconsin; Alameda County, California; and St. Louis, Missouri. They do not, as a whole, provide firm support for the thesis of a litigation explosion.[26]

The question of litigation rates is quite complicated in ways that go beyond methodology or problems of data gathering. To be sure, measurement itself is a serious problem. The fifty states are quite poor at counting their cases, and they have no standard way to classify, count, and report on their caseloads. The statistics they publish are often not very illuminating. It is not always clear how accurate the aggregate figures are, or what story they are really telling about the work of courts.[27] Such broad categories as "contract" cover too many diverse situations to be helpful. Nor does the historical scholarship come close to plugging the gaps in knowledge and understanding.

One of the most illuminating studies of litigation over time was done in Spain. José Juan Toharia studied the formal Spanish courts for the period from 1900 to 1970.[28] He came to a rather startling conclusion. There was no litigation explosion in Spain, even though the period was one of rapid social change and economic expansion. In fact, the volume of cases was in inverse proportion to the rate of modernization. Caseloads (per thousand population) were stagnant or declining, and they showed least growth in the advanced sectors of Spanish society—in big cities like Madrid and Barcelona. Attempts to check Toharia's findings for other places—Italy and Scandinavia, for example—tended to confirm the Spanish experience.[29]

The United States is a more complicated issue. Here, nobody has replicated Toharia's study precisely. The few studies of state courts over time were not primarily interested in volume and caseload; they contain only incidental information on this subject. On the whole, the studies did not find evidence of a litigation explosion in state courts, at least on a long-term basis.

A lot of these studies were bedeviled by the difficulty of defining "litigation." Presumably, the concept should include the work of traffic courts, municipal courts, and small-claims courts; but facts and figures about the work of these basement courts are particularly hard to come by. Even more fundamental is the question of what a "case" is. The easiest thing to count is filings: numbers of complaints entered in court. The trouble is that many filings never turn into a "case" at all, if "case" means a dispute that is *judicially* resolved. Most "cases" filed are dropped before they go to trial.

This is, for example, what happens to most filings in accident and personal injury matters. Insurance companies settle most claims out of court.[30] Of the claims that survive and turn into complaints, most are settled before they actually get to a judge and jury.[31] In California, less than 1 percent of *filed* auto accident claims actually go to trial; the rest are settled along the way.[32]

We need to be clear whether we are interested in filings or actual court dispositions. There is no obvious choice, but the bland fact of slipping a complaint into court hardly accounts for the public excitement about an "explosion." This is not to deny that there are plenty of disputes in society, and that many of them end up in the hands of lawyers. Moreover, there is a lot of "litigation work" that occurs outside of actual trials. Many litigation lawyers spend most of their time on pretrial work—discovery process, for example. These can be hard-fought battles, and they can consume an immense amount of effort and expense. But much of this work is concluded before a judge enters the picture in a decisive way. All of this activity may be part of the broader problem of too much law, but it hardly qualifies as part of the litigation explosion people complain about.

There are other measures that might be meaningful—such as money that is spent on litigation, or that changes hands because of litigation. How much does litigation cost American business? All indications are that the costs are rising. But even these measures do not prove a litigation explosion in the quantitative sense. They are signs of the importance of law and legal process in society—even, perhaps, a growing importance—but not necessarily a sign of exploding litigation.

If we confine ourselves to cases that reach some sort of *outcome* in court, the measurement problem is still rather intractable. Most of these cases are uncontested. In the 1970s, for example, the single biggest category of cases in California's superior courts was divorce (or, to use the newfangled name, petitions for "dissolution of marriage").[33] The overwhelming majority were rubber-stamp affairs. The divorce is not—indeed, cannot be—contested in almost all of these cases. Of course, real disputes between husbands and wives are frequent, and frequently bitter. But the parties and their lawyers usually iron out all the wrinkles before the "case" ever comes to the judge. For all but a few of these family cases, the decree in court is a mere formality. Yet these divorces are "cases" from the statistical standpoint. Other equally cut-and-dried court outcomes—adoptions, name changes, and routine repossessions—also make up a large percentage of the case volume of courts.

Whether litigation is defined as filings in court or as the resolution of actual disputes, it will take careful, systematic work to solve the historical mysteries of litigation rates. The best evidence so far does not suggest that rates have risen sharply in America since the middle of the nineteenth century. Indeed, a case could be made that a far greater proportion of the population was exposed to courts and magistrates in the past than is true today. This seems quite clear as to the colonies in the seventeenth century.[34] It may well be true of the early nineteenth century.[35] From the middle of the nineteenth century on, the rate has been probably falling, although there may have been some rise in the past few years. And it is clear that many people were wailing about a litigation explosion at a time when there was little evidence that rates were rising at all.

On the other hand, to repeat the old saw, where there is smoke, there is fire. There are two quite distinct sorts of "smoke" in this instance. The first is the widespread criticism itself, which suggests a sense of social unease, something gnawing away at the consciousness of some part of the public. What is the underlying cause of this irritation? The second and closely related fact is the impression of a litigation explosion. What is it about the legal system today that gives this impression? Is *something* exploding, even if litigation rates are not? One preliminary answer has already been given: *law* is exploding, in a more general sense. The Toharia study confirms this impression. Toharia did not merely count cases; he also counted notarial acts. In civil-law countries, notaries play a far more important role in the legal system than they do in common-law systems. If you want to form a Spanish corporation, for example, you go to a notary, who draws up the necessary papers.

Toharia's figures on notarial acts stood in striking contrast to those on caseloads. Notarial acts, unlike formal court cases, did not decline over time in Spain; they rose dramatically, and the rise was most pronounced in such big urban and industrial centers as Madrid and Barcelona. The curve for notarial acts, in other words, was exactly the opposite of the curve for court cases. Legal behavior rose steadily in Spain over the years, even where the rate of formal litigation was stagnant or falling.

Even when there is no quantitative explosion, there can be a qualitative one. Perhaps the *number* of cases matters less than the kind of cases and what they deal with. And, indeed, if you clear away the rhetoric surrounding attacks on "hyperlexis," you often find, not that the courts handle too many cases, but that they do too much, and do the wrong things. Too many political, economic, and social issues have been transmuted into litigation; these issues do not belong in court, in the opinion of critics. Once these issues are in the courts, they are handled in the wrong way, at the wrong time, and with the wrong results.[36] In their quest for "perfect justice," the courts have overstepped the mark. They have thus "seriously impaired" their ability to "perform the function for which they were created."[37]

As examples of what is going wrong, there is a fairly standard list of "horribles." Critics often cite some of the more extreme class-action cases—those novel lawsuits, with masses of (nominal) plaintiffs, most of whom may be quite indifferent to the outcome. Or they may object to some sorts of civil rights cases. This category has of course come up almost literally out of nowhere. Before the Civil Rights Act of 1964, civil rights cases were rare indeed. Quite a few of the new civil rights cases are also class actions. Many race and sex discrimination cases are bold in scope, very costly, and deeply unsettling to defendants.

Critics frequently mention as examples of how the system has gone wrong cases that "meddle unduly" in the activities of schools, hospitals, prisons, and business concerns. One of the prime exhibits is *Wyatt v. Stickney*,[38] which intervened in a big way in Alabama's public mental health institutions. A previously mentioned article in a popular magazine refers to the "heavy toll" of litigation on college campuses.[39] It gives as an example a professor's lawsuit against the University of Denver for $19,000,000. He claimed the school "denied him a job" because he was Mexican-American. In a lawsuit for a mere $500,000, another plaintiff charged that Princeton University had suspended him unjustly after accusing him of cheating on a test.

Critics also revel in the occasional odd, freakish lawsuit, which they use to spice up their point that "everybody is suing everybody." Some of these cases are indeed bizarre. One irate man, his ego wounded, threatened to sue a woman who stood him up on a date. An angry young man wanted to sue his mother and father for malpractice; he claimed that their shoddy parenting had made him a nervous wreck.[40] Newspapers, of course, love these eccentric cases. The reader groans and wonders: "what's it all coming to?" The stories reinforce the dominant impression of an endless, pointless blizzard of lawsuits.

What one might call the megacase—the single, monster lawsuit—is another factor that gives rise to this impression of litigation run riot.[41] The great IBM lawsuit was, perhaps, the all-time champion. The federal government filed suit against IBM on January 17, 1969, on the last day of the Johnson administration. The case went on for more than a decade. The suit was brought under the antitrust laws; its purpose was to break up this gigantic company. By 1980, the trial itself had been going on for six years; 9,000 documents had been received into evidence, 100,000 pages of testimony had been transcribed; hundreds of witnesses had testified or given depositions. The case was costing both sides millions of dollars a year. Troops of lawyers were thrown daily into the fray, like young lieutenants at the Battle of Verdun. In the end, the case fizzled into nothing; the Reagan administration simply dropped it. Meanwhile, it had consumed a fantastic amount of legal resources, and evoked an immense amount of comment.

Many private antitrust cases, too, operate on a gigantic scale—the damages sought are in the hundreds of millions, or even billions; lawyers by the carload battle it out; tons of documents are filed; hundreds of witnesses examined; months and months of court time consumed. Yet each of these great lawsuits is (statistically) only a single "case"; the most routine, hackneyed divorce case counts as much. The numbers of these private antitrust suits have risen rapidly in the last generation or so, but the totals are small in comparison to other categories of cases. In 1979, 1,312 such suits were filed in federal court,[42] compared to an average of about one-hundred such cases filed per year in the 1930s and 1940s.[43] Although this represents a colossal 1,000 percent increase, it does not make much of a dent on judicial statistics. On the other hand, it does not take many megacases to create the impression of an explosion. A small herd of elephants attracts more tourists than thousands of mice in the grass.

Still another factor may be this: in contemporary law, as compared to a century ago, no area of life is completely beyond the *potential* reach of law. This explains why the freak cases are even thinkable. (In later chapters this point will be elaborated.) There are fewer and fewer "zones of immunity" from law. People feel, on the whole correctly, that there are few barriers to prevent them from suing other people or institutions, and few barriers to prevent them or their institution from *being* sued. This too creates a feeling that law and litigation are ubiquitous and pervasive.

All of these points, then, may form the basis for the feelings that evoke complaints against the legal system. It is not a quantity explosion, and it is therefore not fair to indict the general population as excessively litigious. Rather, there is a rapid increase in the scope and reach of certain forms of law and a rise in new *kinds* of lawsuits: a qualitative change. Exactly what kind, and why it happened, is the theme of this book.

The Case against the Case against the Law

The preceding pages have expressed doubts about the indictments against the American legal system. Roughly, the charges were these: there is too much law, there are too many lawyers, and there is too much litigation; all this produces economic waste, perverts justice, and interferes with efficiency and order, both public and private. There is, to be sure, no single, consistent "case" against the law, and some of the accusations tend to cancel each other out. For example, people say that lawyers are tricksters who prevent people from getting what is rightfully theirs. At the same time, lawyers are accused of the opposite sin. They use the law to get more benefits for people than they deserve. Dangerous criminals go free on "technicalities"; corporate malefactors are let off the hook. Lawyers both prevent redress and promote excessive redress. Of course, it is possible for lawyers to be guilty of both these offenses; it is possible that crooks and malefactors benefit from legalism, while good citizens are shut out of the process.

This book assumes a more complex reality, and the following chapters will try to spell out some details. It is worth mentioning, too, that not everybody agrees that there is too much law and lawyering. Some argue that there is, in many regards, too little. Such a view is at the heart of the movement to improve access to justice by making the legal system less formal, less legalistic, and more open to the general public.[44] This movement claims that the "big boys" (government, big corporations, big unions) get away with murder because they alone command legal talent; there are too few lawyers for poor people and underdogs, and litigation is too costly and slow for most people. Laura Nader writes that one of the "greatest challenges facing the legal profession" is to "create forums that can resolve disputes between distant, unequal parties with both fairness and credibility."[45] This complaint is not inconsistent with the general charges against the legal profession and the legal system; Nader would not welcome vast additions to the ranks of corporate lawyers, but she *would* welcome lawyers who met the needs of ordinary people.

Then there are those who feel that the amount of legal action in our society is about right, or at least that it is moving in the right direction. After all, a strong case can be made that the legal system has lost a good deal of its narrowness and rigidity. The system is certainly more sensitive to the needs of racial minorities, for example, than was true in any earlier period. People are in general better able to redress grievances than they were a century ago. The concept of due process has permeated institutions that were once, in important ways, quite lawless—immune from what would now be considered rudimentary measures of fairness. There is a literature, partly normative and partly descriptive, on the movement toward a "responsive" or "reflexive" legal system.[46] At the very least, a process seems to be unfolding that is causing a real change in society: the "due process revolution." A later chapter takes up this theme.

Critics of the legal system also often assume that more rules and laws are undesirable because they mean less freedom for the individual. Actually, the relationship between personal liberty and the volume of rules and regulations is tangled and complex. Take, for example, the impact of the automobile on law and on life. The automobile has been the occasion for an immense amount of law: traffic rules, rules about drunk driving, rules about auto safety, drivers' license laws, and the like. Much of this is new law, or so completely made over from horse-and-buggy law (traffic rules, for example), that it might as well be thought of as new.

A heavier load of law burdens the automobile driver, then, than ever burdened the drivers of carriages or riders of horses. But is it *felt* as a burden? Some of it is absolutely necessary, and people realize as much. When millions of people own machines that can go over one hundred miles per hour, some control of speed and traffic is unavoidable. But in addition—and this is the crucial point—the new rules and institutions are part of the price of an automotive society, and in an automotive society ordinary people have a kind of freedom of mobility that their ancestors could not imagine in their wildest dreams. Is the automotive society less free than a society in which people were born, lived, and died in a single spot; where they were chained to their land, their village, their hut?

An even more fundamental problem exists with most standard criticisms of the legal system: the critics seem blind to the facts of social life in the United States. Their criticism rests, usually implicitly, on theories of law and society that are questionable, if not downright wrong.

The critics assume, generally speaking, that in some way or other law and legal institutions play a leading role in American society. (Curiously enough, this is also a problem with some of the main defenses of the system.) If there are 650,000 lawyers, and if this is "too much," then the lawyers must be doing great damage. As I said, the critics somehow forget supply and demand. The supply of lawyers is treated as if it appeared by magic, or through some weird pathology of the market. If bright young people flock into law schools, they do so because they recognize a demand for their services. And they may be basically right.

Some lawyers no doubt make trouble, stir up litigation, and foment conflict, all to make business for themselves. But on the whole, lawyers do not lead; they follow. The demand for their services comes from outside the legal system. If there is a breakdown of trust in society, if social cohesion has eroded, this is not to be laid at the lawyers' doors. These diseases of the social order, if real, precede the work of the lawyers, and indeed are the immediate source of the demand for their work.

Even the most obvious sins of the lawyers, the dirtiest, dingiest corners of legal practice, are in their own ways responses to social demand. Take, for example, the history of ambulance chasing—not a chapter of professional history anybody is particularly proud of. As far as one can tell, ambulance chasing became the subject of talk in the late nineteenth century. The *Dictionary of Americanisms* traces the term to 1897. An ambulance chaser runs after ambulances or rushes into hospital rooms or funeral parlors, looking for likely plaintiffs; lawyers may do this dirty work themselves, or hire others to do it for them. The point is to drum up personal injury business. To most segments of the bar, ambulance chasers are the lowest of the low.

Nobody is minded to defend the ambulance chaser, but this low-life among lawyers did not spring up out of nowhere. First of all, there was a vast increase in personal injury in the late nineteenth century. This was especially true of street injuries—caused by electric railways, for example, and later by automobiles and trucks. The phenomenon is also connected with the rise of the insurance business. The ambulance-chasing lawyer was reacting to ambulance-chasing insurance companies. Claims agents were every bit as unscrupulous as lawyers. They tried to rush to the victim or his family first, hoping to get a signed release of claims, before the lawyers arrived. One writer called these agents "kindred" of the ambulance chasers: "As bad as is the practice of soliciting law business for large contingent fees, surely the preying on the weak and helpless, the poor and ignorant, is as much if not more deserving of condemnation."[47] Specific practices of insurance companies and tortfeasors called ambulance chasing into being, and late nineteenth-century tort law was its immediate background.

There may be dozens of crooked lawyers, but patterns of crookedness invite some sort of explanation outside the system, or at least outside the profession. Lawyers (and judges) participated in the hypocrisy and perjury of divorce practice before the days of no-fault.[48] But they were trapped between an enormous demand for consensual divorce and a sociolegal system that, for various reasons, preferred a collusive system. When consensual divorce was legitimated, one whole class of shady lawyer passed into history.

To understand what is happening inside the legal system, it is best to start from the outside, by looking at great general movements of social force. America has made the legal system what it is; the legal system has not made America. Of course there is mutual influence, but the main lines of cause run from society to the law, not the other way around. Lawyers and jurists tend to assume naively that important legal events always begin inside the world of the jurists, even when they have significant "outside" consequences. It does not in any way take away from the meaning of law—a mighty presence in society—to posit the social dependence of law as an axiom. In some regard, all studies of law as a social phenomenon presuppose this axiom, or at least treat it with great respect. It is also a matter of observable fact. We *see* society making law every day in courts, legislatures, and agencies.

The social dependence of law also casts some doubt on the notion that there is some sort of independent "crisis" in the legal system, separate from any general social crisis. If legal systems are bound to the rhythms of particular societies, it is difficult, on principle, to accept the idea that law is subject to major fits and spasms of its own. It is more plausible to assume that fits and spasms going on in society are echoed in the legal system.

But modern legal and social thought is rife with discussion of a "crisis" in legal systems. Some scholars link it to broader, more general crises in the very structure of society. Particularly among European scholars, there is talk about a "legitimation crisis"; this is connected in turn to the idea that the welfare state has become "ungovernable," partly because of excessive expectations and demands.[49]

The literature on the modern crisis is rich and difficult, and most of it does not touch directly on the legal system. There are, however, some important points of contact. One is the assumption, underlying much of the literature, that the welfare state has been stretched beyond its capacity to function. This theory of overload has been applied as well to the legal system,[50] and it has obvious affinities with the debate and unease over the litigation explosion.

It is not clear, however, what it means to say that problems are beyond the "capacity" of a legal system. There are certainly problems that no society has been able to solve very well, but I know of none whose special brand of insolubility can be labeled as "legal." The "capacity" of a legal system is limitless. A problem is beyond the capacity of law only if it is beyond the capacity of society, period. But the literature assumes that in some way the distinction between the legal and nonlegal realm makes problematic the "capacity" of law to do society's bidding. Perhaps the only way to make sense of the argument is by referring back to the literature on the "nature" of courts and other institutions. Many legal scholars, and especially those of the so-called legal process school,[51] assume that the choice of institutional forms makes a crucial difference to American law. When courts, for example, step outside of their "inherent" functions, they risk ruin for themselves, for society, or both.

But this is essentially a normative idea masquerading as a statement of fact. Courts (and all other institutions) constantly change their functions, capacities, roles, and habits. There is no more an enduring "inherent" function or power of a court than there is an "inherent" function of a king.[52]

On Legal Autonomy

Views about whether or not there is a crisis in the legal system are connected with the view of the law or legal system that the particular scholar starts with. The crux of the matter is to decide to what extent the legal system is autonomous. Is each and every essential trait of the legal system determined by outside social forces, or is the system a tough, self-contained entity, evolving and unfolding according to its own internal norms and rules?

This is an ancient, and to some extent a fruitless, debate. Every scholar worth his salt would agree that the legal system has *some* autonomy; the question is, how much? Every scholar, similarly, would admit that the outside world affects the legal system; again the question is, how much? One could imagine a kind of continuum; at one pole is a concept of law as totally autonomous; at the other, a concept of law as totally dependent on society. Probably no jurist of any importance would be located at either extreme, although some would lean much more to one side, some to the other.

The basic bent of social scientists and their fellow travelers in legal scholarship is toward the "social" end of the continuum. The basic bent of orthodox legal scholars is toward the "autonomous" end. Ultimately, these are matters of ideology. Nothing can be really proved. It is often possible to show fairly clearly that social forces lie behind some particular legal development. But to make the total case goes beyond human science.

There are signs of renewed interest in the idea of an autonomous legal system. The modern forms of this concept are a good deal subtler than those of nineteenth-century legal thought. They may rest (as in the work of Niklas Luhmann) on concepts and structures drawn from organizational sociology or systems theory.[53] Autonomy is an attractive idea to some scholars because they feel that human beings need legal autonomy. That is, only an autonomous legal system can avoid knuckling under to the state; such a system is not, as Teubner argues, "reducible to a set of decisions determined by power relations, organization structures, professional roles, and the like."[54] The legal systems of totalitarian states are, alas, never autonomous. The naked power of the elite who run these countries overrides or transforms the law.

But this argument, I believe, confuses two different things: structural independence and autonomy. The United States Supreme Court, for example, is highly independent—the judges serve for life, and the regime cannot pressure them in any obvious way. The Court can, and often does, defy the government at will. What could be more independent than the decision in *U.S. v. Nixon*, which helped drive a president from office?[55] But independence does not make the court "autonomous," in the sense of a "social institution, whose development depends on its own internal dynamics."[56] The court is insulated from the *regime*; but this does not mean that its behavior is not responsive to social forces, either directly, or as filtered through the value systems of judges. At the very least, one cannot infer "autonomy" from structural independence.

To a degree, the quarrel between autonomists and antiautonomists is a quarrel over words and definitions. Indeed, a definition of law is crucial to the argument. To those most concerned with the "crisis" in the legal system, "law" conjures up essentially those parts of the system that one might call "lawyer's law"; that is, ideas, problems, or situations that (whatever their status as living law) are interesting to legal theorists. Legal logic, debates among scholars—these seem to make a great deal of difference in the way "nice" little problems are shaped, problems that engage attention in law schools and law books. This is a standpoint that is fundamentally law-centered; from this vantage point, it is easy to think of the legal system as autonomous. If, on the other hand, "law" or the "legal system" includes all of what I have called legal acts—the rules and regulations of the modern state, the processes of administrative governance, police behavior—and what I have called legal behavior—including the work of lawyers in their offices, advising clients—then the influence of the whole social order on the way the legal system works seems much more pervasive, the boundaries blur, and the autonomy of law shrinks to the merest wisp.

To some extent, choosing a definition of law is a matter of convenience or logical coherence. I choose the expanded definition, and a conception of law that makes it easier to assume that the outside world plays the dominant role in molding law. An expanded definition shifts the focus away from a strictly legal "crisis"; any "crisis" within the system simply reflects "crisis" outside the system, no more and no less.

Legitimacy and Its Discontents

Juergen Habermas, for one, has popularized the idea of a "legitimation" crisis.[57] The concept comes in various forms and guises. One focus is on the moral or normative authority of law, and its (assumed) breakdown in modern society. One cannot talk about a "legitimation crisis" without defining terms. The core idea is that an invisible glue called legitimacy holds a society together. Legitimacy is a theory about the rightness of those people and institutions that actually govern; the belief prevents anarchy and induces most people to obey orders and commands without the use of force.

The literature on legitimacy and legitimation leaves a lot to be desired, and the very concept has been criticized, notably by Alan Hyde.[58] It does seem likely that scholars overestimate the strength and value of legitimacy as a factor in social "integration." Hyde surely goes too far; he tries to get rid of the concept of legitimacy altogether. But the word describes real attitudes, held by real people, in real societies. To be sure, it is not easy to prove what these attitudes are, and how they are changing. Public opinion polls provide some support for the notion that people believe in the rightness of institutions; at least people tend to think that familiar institutions are natural or inevitable or invincible. It is plausible (though the evidence here is quite poor) that these beliefs affect behavior. Legitimacy, in short, is part of the legal culture, if it is anything.

In some ways, arguments about a legitimation crisis, or about the overload of legal institutions, can be turned upside down. Hardly anybody thinks that Americans in the 1980s are on the verge of rebellion. Nobody expects a military coup, or a wave of bread riots, or peasant revolts, or mobs storming the White House. If Americans overuse "law," this is more plausibly a tribute to the strength of legitimacy, than it is a sign of crisis, a sign of the tottering of temples.

But I would not care to press this point too far. And ideas about right and wrongs, about legitimacy, about authority, about justice, about law, are complex and mutable. They can and do change over time, with changing social conditions.

Total Justice and Legal Culture

But to return to the thesis: it is obvious that gigantic changes have taken place in modern legal systems as well as in modern social systems. These reflect, in part, changes in the modern state; and in part, they help create vast changes in the state. If Jefferson or Lincoln—or even Theodore Roosevelt—came back to life, he would hardly recognize the American government. He would be, in particular, dazzled by its size and scope. The total budget of a state like Massachusetts, around 1800, was something on the order of $100,000; the total receipts of the federal government in 1800 were $10,849,000.[59] Even if one takes population growth and inflation into account, the increase is fantastic. In 1984, the Defense Department alone spends more in an hour than the whole government took in in 1800.

These changes in the modern state are by definition changes in or through law. The activities of the modern state are in each case constituted by statutes, orders, institutions, processes, or patterns of behavior which are "legal," even under restrictive definitions of that word. Changes in the scope and scale of government are also organically connected with changes in the rules and processes of what is sometimes called "private" law—ordinary contract law, family law, tort law, and rules about real estate. The domains of both "public" and "private" law have expanded, and in a particular way—in the direction of what is called, in this book, total justice.

These two parallel developments are joined, and influence each other, in a complicated interactive process. The precise interconnections have not always been well explored. In part, this is because scholarship tends to divide the law into separate little boxes or categories. People who specialize in government or public law do not link their work to that of those who write about torts, or the law of landlord and tenant.

The interactive process is, of course, too complicated to describe in simple terms. But the point is this: social change leads to change in legal culture; this influences the demands that people place on the state and the legal system. The state cannot help but react, one way or another, to these demands. The responses, in turn, produce further changes, further demands, in a process that (so far) seems to have no logical end.

The key concept here is *legal culture*: the ideas, attitudes, values, and opinions about law held by people in a society.[60] The assumption is that these ideas and attitudes influence legal behavior, especially the level of demands placed on the legal system. Legal culture, then, is a "network of values and attitudes . . . which determines when and why and where people turn to law or government or turn away."[61] It is thus the immediate source of legal change, whatever the ultimate source may be. Legal culture is not well explored as an object of research, but there does seem to be a growing interest in the subject.[62]

More specifically, my argument is framed in terms of certain great changes that have taken place in world history. These changes are summed up in such catch phrases as "the Industrial Revolution" or "the rise of the welfare-regulatory state." Such phrases may conceal more than they explain; they cover up a huge amount of complexity and variance. But the general line of development seems reasonably clear.

For centuries, the world in a sense turned slowly on its axis. Social change is inevitable, but in many societies it moved (from the modern standpoint) at a snail's pace. People lived out their lives in the iron grip of tradition, in a rigid but comfortable prison of habits and norms. The great adventure began with those interlocking changes, boiling up out of Europe, that brought the machine age, the factory age, the age of roaring technology—the process called modernization. The small, narrow world of villages, woods, and fields was brutally and rapidly converted into the world as we know it today, a world of giant enterprises, high technology, and crowded cities.

Whatever brought these changes about in the first place, the results have been truly revolutionary. Not only do people talk, live, earn money, and eat differently, they also think differently; the way they look at the world, their ideology, culture, and outlook have been transformed. The modern personality is distinctively different from the old-fashioned or peasant mentality.[63]

Of course, there is no such thing as *the* legal culture, or *the* legal personality. In a country as large and diverse as the United States, there are all sorts of attitudes and opinions about law. Nevertheless, certain gross changes in legal culture can be tracked over the past century or so. The changes seem to be going in a single direction, though of course with zigs and zags: greater penetration of the legal order into affairs of life and state. In 1985, citizens of this country do not stand apart from the legal order; they confront it directly. They feel its impact more and more, and they turn to it with more and more requests and demands. This is the essence of the law explosion.

The level of demands on the system has been rising steadily over the years. And the system, since it is not autonomous, not insulated from social pressure, must respond to the demands. Whether it responds adequately or efficiently or well is another question. "Respond" is one of those dangerous words that has two meanings, too close to each other for comfort. Like "luck," which means both good luck and luck in general, whether good or bad, a "response" can mean a favorable, satisfying response or it can mean any reaction, good or bad. A sharp "no" and a slap on the wrist are responses; so is throwing tear gas cannisters at protesters. The word is used here in its broader meaning: *any* response.

The legal system, then, always responds to demands, but it often responds by saying no to particular claims or pressures; just as often, if not more so, it says maybe, or says something contradictory or unintelligible. In a sense, it is even unrealistic (though necessary) to talk about the legal system "responding" to a "demand" from some relevant public. The legal system is part of the general culture, the general political system, the general economy. The boundaries between its domain and the general social order are hopelessly blurred.

Nonetheless, it makes sense to talk in some contexts about demands on the legal system and about responses that take the form of legal acts. Certainly there are historical patterns of responses. The modern Western countries, including the United States, are open systems; that is, systems with channels through which demands can reach authorities. These channels are not open to everybody, since none of these countries are pure democracies, nor are the channels open all the time; but they do exist. Hence, the system says yes to some people some of the time, though never all of the people all of the time. "Yes" is more frequent when the people making demands have power, wealth, or prestige.

This is also a country with a large middle-class mass. It began its historical career in a situation of abundance of land. It began as a colony, but imperial control was at first quite weak. A much broader class of people had a stake in the economy through ownership of capital than was true of England or of other countries. This enormous middle class has always exercised great economic and political power.[64] Whether or not there is a ruling elite in this country, the middle class clearly has power to achieve at least some of its demands from the state. And responses from the state (and law) have fed expectations, which in turn have led to still greater demands. There is, then, a kind of spiral, coiling in the direction of more and more law, more and more state intervention.

This in itself can produce in outside observers a definite sense of crisis. The observer looks at the system and sees rising expectations. The state keeps growing and growing. Welfare and regulatory burdens mount higher and higher. Taxes take a greater and greater share of national income. Surely, the observer thinks, there comes a point where high taxation and overregulation will kill the goose with the golden eggs. The system is bound to collapse of its excess weight. In the 1970s, stagnant economies and deep recession fed this sense of unease. Many welfare systems—in such countries as Denmark and Holland—seemed badly overextended.

The doom and gloom may or may not be justified. It is hard to avoid the fallacy of extrapolation: expecting the future to be like the past, only more so. But only one thing is certain about the future, and that is uncertainty. With regard to social change, or population growth, or national income, future developments will definitely not look like straight lines on a graph. It is true that the process just described has been going on for a century or more, feeding on itself, and spiraling upward and onward. But nobody knows the "laws" (if any) that govern its growth. The line may level off, or even turn back. The oil crisis of the 1970s and the recession that followed brought about some anguished reappraisal in the welfare states. Many European countries (and the United States) tried to cut back social programs. This trend may or may not continue.

Still, the evolution up to now has been impressive, and it has led to a new form of legal culture. The next chapters deal with this subject.

NOTES

1. Juergen Habermas, *Legitimationsprobleme im Spaetkapitalismus* (1975), p. 11.

2. For a discussion and critique, see Philippe C. Schmitter, "Interest Intermediation and Regime Governability in Contemporary Western Europe and North America," in Suzanne D. Berger, ed., *Organizing Interests in Western Europe: Pluralism, Corporatism, and the Transformation of Politics* (1981), p. 287.

3. See, for example, Wolfgang Seibel, " 'Gesetzesflut,' Konservative Staatsrechtslehre und Kritische Sozialwissenschaft," *Demokratie und Recht* (1980), p. 123.

4. Gerald W. Gawalt, *The Promise of Power: the Emergence of the Legal Profession in Massachusetts, 1760–1840* (1979), p.14.

5. Albert P. Blaustein and Charles O. Porter, *The American Lawyer, A Summary of the Survey of the Legal Profession* (1954), pp. 2–6.

6. B. Peter Pashigian, "The Number and Earnings of Lawyers: Some Recent Findings," *American Bar Foundation Research Journal* (1978):51.

7. See Marc Galanter, "Reading the Landscape of Disputes: What We Know and Don't Know (and Think We Know) about our Allegedly Contentious and Litigious Society," *UCLA Law Review* 31 (1983):4.

8. For an example of the use of this term, see Wayne D. Brazil, "Civil Discovery: Lawyers' Views of Its Effectiveness, Its Principal Problems and Abuses," *American Bar Association Research Journal* (1980):787, 825.

9. See, for example, Heinz Eulau and John D. Sprague, *Lawyers in Politics: A Study in Professional Convergence* (1964); Justin J. Green, John R. Schmidhauser, Larry L. Berg, and David Brady, "Lawyers in Congress: A New Look at Some Old Assumptions," *Western Political Q.* 26 (1973):440.

10. Robert A. Kagan and Robert Rosen, "On the Social Significance of Large Law Firms," Conference paper, Stanford Law School, Feb. 24, 1984.

11. James Driscoll, *California's Legislature* (1976), p. 171.

12. Donald Black, *The Behavior of Law* (1976), p. 2.

13. Lawrence M. Friedman, "Limited Monarchy: the Rise and Fall of Student Rights," in *School Days, Rule Days* (in press, 1985).

14. See the Education of the Handicapped Act, 20 U.S.C.A. sec. 1400ff.

15. Lawrence M. Friedman, *The Legal System: A Social Science Perspective* (1975), p. 4.

16. Ibid., pp. 4–5.

17. See, for example, James Buchanan and Gordon Tullock, *The Calculus of Consent* (1961).

18. On the reality (or not) of the litigation explosion, see Lawrence M. Friedman, "The Six Million Dollar Man: Litigation and Rights Consciousness in Modern America," *Maryland L. Rev.* 39 (1980):661. The literature is reviewed in Galanter, "Reading the Landscape." Victor Flango et al., *The Business of State Trial Courts* (1983) presents data on recent years; some of the figures suggest more reality to the "explosion" than most other studies of the subject, with regard to the 1970s at least; but see Galanter, "Reading the Landscape," pp. 40–41, n. 174, on the interpretation of these figures.

19. *Changing Times* (April 1983), p. 76.

20. Bayless Manning, "Hyperlexis: Our National Disease," *Nwn. U. L. Rev.* 71 (1977):767.

21. Jethro K. Lieberman, *The Litigious Society* (1981). Similarly, Jerrold Auerbach begins his study of dispute settlement in American history, *Justice without Law? Resolving Disputes without Lawyers* (1983), with the statement that Americans "belong to the most legalistic and litigious society in the world" (p. 3). He presents no evidence to support this statement, and the book itself is about alternatives to litigation. The book is especially good on the relationship between legal and general culture.

22. *U.S. News & World Report* (December 20, 1982), p. 58.

23. For the figures, see David S. Clark, "Adjudication to Administration: A Statistical Analysis of Federal District Courts in the Twentieth Century," *So. Cal. L. Rev.* 55:65 (1981).

24. For the work of the National Center for State Courts, see Flango et al., *The Business of State Trial Courts.*

25. See Galanter, "Reading the Landscape," pp. 51–61.

26. The literature is summed up in Lawrence M. Friedman, "Courts over Time," in K. Boyum and L. Mather, eds., *Empirical Theories About Courts* (1983), pp. 9, 17–23; and in Galanter, "Reading the Landscape."

27. On the problems of measurement and the deficiencies of reporting, see the report of the National Center for State Courts, *State Court Caseload Statistics: The State of the Art* (1978).

28. José Juan Toharia, *Cambio Social y Vida Juridica en Espana* (1974).

29. See Britt-Mari P. Blegvad et al., *Arbitration as a Means of Solving Conflicts* (1973), pp. 103–105.

30. This point emerges clearly from the various studies of the work of trial courts. See, in general, Ralph Cavanagh and Austin Sarat, "Thinking about Courts: Toward and Beyond a Jurisprudence of Judicial Competence," *Law & Society Review* 14 (1980):371.

31. The process is described in H. Laurence Ross, *Settled Out of Court: the Social Process of Insurance Claims Adjustment* (1970).

32. Mark A. Peterson and George L. Priest, *The Civil Jury, Trends in Trials and Verdicts, Cook County, Illinois, 1960–1979* (1982), p. 1.

33. See Lawrence M. Friedman and Robert V. Percival, "A Tale of Two Courts: Litigation in Alameda and San Benito Counties," *Law & Society Review* 10 (1976):167.

34. See George B. Curtis, "The Colonial County Court, Social Forum and Legislative Precedent, Accomack County, Virginia, 1633–1639," *Va. Mag. of Hist. and Biog.* 85 (1977):274; see also David L. Konig, *Law and Society in Puritan Massachusetts, Essex County, 1629–1692* (1979). It has to be recalled that the county courts of colonial periods were busy places that did a lot of things besides the work we associate with courts. For descriptions, see Hendrik Hartog, "The Public Law of a County Court: Judicial Government in Eighteenth Century Massachusetts," *Am. J. Legal Hist.* 20 (1976):282; William E. Nelson, *Dispute and Conflict Resolution in Plymouth County, Massachusetts, 1725–1825* (1981). To get a fairer comparison, perhaps one would have to ask what percentage of the population of an American county in any given year goes to court in any capacity (juror, witness), or is exposed to court process (including traffic court), or is involved with local zoning, taxing, or probate authorities; or registers a deed, gets married, or the like. Probably the seventeenth and eighteenth centuries still win, but by a reduced margin.

35. See Joseph G. Baldwin, *The Flush Times of Alabama and Mississippi* (1853), p. 240.

36. Donald L. Horowitz, *The Courts and Social Policy* (1977).

37. Macklin Fleming, *The Price of Perfect Justice* (1974), p. 169.

38. 344 F. Supp. 387 (M.D. Ala. 1972); 503 Fed. 2d 1305 (5th Cir., 1974). There was a finding that mentally ill patients, civilly committed to public institutions, have a constitutional right to some sort of treatment; and the courts were willing to go rather far in deciding what kind of regime was minimally acceptable at the institutions.

39. *U.S. News & World Report* (December 20, 1982), p. 59.

40. *Washington Post* (Aug. 18, 1980), p. 1, col. 2; *New York Times* (June 16, 1980), p. 16, col. 2.

41. See Marc Galanter, "Mega-Law and Mega-Lawyering in the Contemporary United States," in R. Dingwall and P. Lewis, eds., *The Sociology of the Professions: Lawyers, Doctors and Others* (1983), p. 152.

42. 1979 *Admin. Off. U.S. Cts. Ann. Rep.*, p. 62.

43. Richard Posner, *Antitrust Law: An Economic Perspective* (1976), p. 34.

44. There is a large literature on the access to justice movement. See Mauro Cappelletti and Bryant Garth, "Access to Justice: the Worldwide Movement to Make Rights Effective: A General Report," in M. Cappelletti and B. Garth, eds., *Access to Justice, Vol. I* (1978), p. 3.

45. Laura Nader, "Alternatives to the American Judicial System," in L. Nader, ed., *No Access to Law* (1980), p. 49.

46. Philippe Nonet and Philip Selznick, *Law and Society in Transition: Toward Responsive Law* (1978); Gunther Teubner, "Substantive and Reflexive Elements in Modern Law," *Law & Society Review,* 17 (1983):239.

47. Minor Bronaugh, "The Ambulance Chaser vs. the Claim Agent," *Law Notes* 24 (October 1920):126, 127.

48. See Nelson M. Blake, *The Road to Reno, A History of Divorce in the United States* (1962); Lawrence M. Friedman, "Rights of Passage: Divorce Law in Historical Perspective," *Oregon Law Review,* forthcoming, 1985.

49. For a critique of this point of view, see Schmitter, "Interest Intermediation and Regime Governability."

50. See Teubner, "Substantive and Reflexive Elements."

51. The leading text is Henry M. Hart and Albert M. Sacks, *The Legal Process* (tentative edition, 2 volumes 1958) (never really published; but found in many libraries, in mimeographed form, and an influential teaching tool); see G. Edward White, "The Evolution of Reasoned Elaboration: Jurisprudential Criticism and Social Change," *Virginia Law Review* 59 (1973):279ff., especially p. 290.

52. Lawrence M. Friedman, "Legal Rules and the Process of Social Change," *Stanford L. Rev.* 19 (1967):786, 798.

53. Niklas Luhmann, *Ausdifferenzierung des Rechts* (1981), especially ch. 2.

54. Teubner, "Substantive and Reflexive Elements," p.247.

55. 418 U.S. 683 (1974).

56. Teubner, "Substantive and Reflexive Elements," p.247.

57. The reference is to Juergen Habermas's well-known book, *Legitimation Crisis* (1975).

58. See Alan Hyde, "The Concept of Legitimation in the Sociology of Law," *Wisconsin Law Review* (1983):380.

59. *Historical Statistics of the United States*, Vol. II, p. 1106 (1975).

60. Friedman, *The Legal System*, p. 194.

61. Lawrence M. Friedman, "Legal Culture and Social Development," *Law & Society Review* 4 (1969):29.

62. For an overview of the American literature, see Austin Sarat, "Studying American Legal Culture: an Assessment of Survey Research," *Law & Society Review* 11 (1977):427.

63. Alex Inkeles and David H. Smith, *Becoming Modern, Individual Change in Six Developing Countries* (1974).

64. See David M. Potter, *People of Plenty: Economic Abundance and the American Character* (1965); Lawrence M. Friedman, *A History of American Law* (1973), pp. 99–100.

3

THE BIRTH
OF A MODERN
LEGAL CULTURE

T HE CENTRAL PROPOSITION of this book is that social change leads to changes in legal culture, which in turn produce legal change. What has happened, in the last century or so, to American legal culture?

A few words should be said at the outset about modern society, which I will contrast with two other types of society. All three types are idealized constructs, exaggerated for purposes of argument. No human society is simple, although some are more complex than others. Societies are also, in a way, always both logical and illogical. Their features and behavior patterns are coherent and form definite cultures. But at the same time, all societies are illogical in many ways. They have not been deliberately and rationally designed; rather, they simply evolve, and not with an eye to fitting into little boxes social scientists contrive.

Traditional society ranges from hunters and gatherers all the way to relatively sophisticated communities in medieval Europe. All these societies, however, have certain traits in common. Primary groups—

people in face-to-face contact—dominate social existence. Tradition rules most areas of life, and governs much of a person's behavior. Most norms of conduct are unwritten; people learn them without going to school, and follow them without threat of the policeman's club. Public opinion is a powerful force, molding behavior and reinforcing the old ways of life.

There has been much discussion of the role of law in traditional societies. Some societies have so little formal structure that it is hard to identify anything like a legal system.[1] Other traditional societies do have courts, judges, mediators, and even jails.[2] Traditional societies make heavy use of punishments that enlist public opinion; punishments that emphasize shame, for example. The pillory and the stocks of Puritan Massachusetts are famous instances.

Traditional societies are tight and close-knit; they are extremely *social*. At the other end of the scale would be a society (if one could call it that) made up entirely of isolated individuals or families, completely self-sufficient, a law unto themselves. Man is a social animal, and in a pure form no "society" of absolute individuals can exist. It is not normal for people to live outside of communities, even in isolated family units. The American frontiersman, as conventionally pictured, was about as close as anyone could get to life in a society of isolates. There were some people who deliberately avoided cities and towns, living in log cabins in the wilderness, far from civilization. They grew or caught their own food; the women made clothing for the family out of homegrown materials; the family lived entirely on its own; husband and wife educated their children; they did not form part of a larger "society" in most senses of that word.

Modern society, in some ways, falls between these two societal types. As in a traditional society, people live in communities and depend upon others. For the most part, people live in family groups or in close networks of friends. Their most important relationships are face-to-face, intense relationships with family, coworkers, and friends.

Psychologically, however, many people look to the frontiersman (or their image of the frontiersman) as a model: the independent person, the radical individualist not beholden to anybody, the person who lives life as he or she sees fit, the free spirit, the nonconformist. Moreover, the country is big, the population is mobile, and it is easy to break loose from one's primary group, choose a new life and identity, and start over in a new place. This was almost impossible in traditional society. Modern man (or woman), then, can at least *think* about radical individualism, though few ever get as far as to act out that fantasy.

Mostly this is because people cannot tolerate a truly isolated life. Few have the skills to make it on their own; most of us would not last a week, in a wilderness. The closest we can come is a more or less rootless, isolated life in the city; this too takes its toll. But quite apart from what isolation costs psychologically, the conditions of modern life foster dependence. The characteristic trait of modern society is enormous division of labor. Each person has his or her own tasks. People do not grow their own food, weave their own clothes, educate their own children, heal their own wounds. We do what we are trained to do, and rely on others for the rest.

In this kind of society, there is a feature unknown to traditional society: extraordinary dependence on people we do not know, never meet, never see. Food and clothing are made by strangers in factories and processing plants and bought in stores. People move into houses that somebody else builds, to specifications the buyer may not understand. In a sense, then, the typical person has no control over the basic necessities of life. There are no personal guarantees that the applesauce in this jar is healthy or wholesome, or even that it is made out of apples. There is no way to guarantee that the elevator in a downtown building is safe enough to carry the passengers' weight. We do not know the people who actually design, make, and market our goods, or who check and maintain them; hence, there is no way to be sure that informal norms will control these people.

There *are* controls of course. There is, for example, the invisible hand of the market. This goes a long way toward replacing informal norms in regulating conduct. The market, or the theory of the market, was historically also seen as a mode of control good enough to replace the old absolutist states of Europe, and a prime reason for dismantling their governments in favor of the liberal state. Some economists believe that the market is a kind of magic; that attempts to regulate the economy or intervene in its workings will almost always do more harm than good. Perhaps; but most people do not accept this orthodoxy whole hog; even in the heyday of laissez faire, there was dissent and debate.[3] People doubt that the market exerts enough control; they refuse to rely on it as the sole way of preventing food poisoning, for example, or as a guarantee that trains and planes will not crash, or that nobody starves in the streets.

To protect people from the harm that can come from modern society and its tools—on which they are totally dependent—some new, more powerful method of control is needed. This means intervention by some strong outside force, a force that can control harm at its source. In short, what is needed is the generalized third party, the state. Or to put it still another way, what is needed is law. If custom is the name given to norms that govern face-to-face relationships, then law is the name for formal, authoritative norms that come from the state and govern the relationships among strangers. It stands in contrast both to the informal norms of traditional society and to the despotic or charismatic norms of absolutist states.

Of course, this does not exhaust the possible meanings or functions of "law." As mentioned, there are definitions of law broad enough to cover norms in tribal societies, too, not to mention norms of feudalism or of Oriental despotism. But for present purposes, I want to emphasize a different aspect of the legal: its formality, its relationship to organized government and to authority—in short, to the modern state.

One point, however, should be made clear. Dependence on strangers is a strong feature of modern life, but this does not necessarily mean that people in modern society feel helpless and lost. They may or may not. Does the tribesman in the bush, who catches, kills, and eats wild animals, whose wife gathers berries and grubs and makes loincloths out of plant fibers, feel a greater sense of control, more power to make his own destiny, than a secretary in Phoenix, Arizona, or a foreman in a Pittsburgh steel mill? Probably not. The cosmos of foremen and secretaries is not a seething mass of demons, a whirlwind of mysterious forces that nobody understands, and around which they weave all sorts of myths. Modern workers may feel politically helpless or anomic in all sorts of ways, but they respect science and believe in its power. With regard to the realms of both nature and man, workers are confident that meaningful outside control is indeed possible.

This point is central to the argument here. The steelworker in Pittsburgh has no personal control over the way peas are processed and put in cans. The secretary has no personal control over the way a pilot flies a DC-10. But they are sure that there are ways to control both the canner and the pilot. They think, in other words, that society has the knowledge and means to prevent botulism and avoid plane crashes; the only trick is making sure the right machinery is used, at the right time, and in the right place. It is for these purposes that they, and society in general, turn to law.

The argument, thus, runs as follows: by the nineteenth century, at the latest, a new kind of society had developed in the West: the society of technology, industry, science, machines. Science and machines gave people tremendous control over time, distance, and destiny. This period was followed by the age of modern medicine; then came the age of the computer. Each advance in science and technology seemed to increase the possibility of control—over nature, over the conditions of life.[4] But control always required regulation, rules, implementation; control was, and had to be, vested in law, legal process, and the state.

And vested it was. The period of the Industrial Revolution began with a vision of small government—a reaction against the pervasive, despotic state. Yet it ended up as the period of a new Leviathan. Governments—and law—grew to vast, epic size; in many countries these are still in process of growth. In the early nineteenth century, scholars and jurists understood "law" in a rather narrow, technical sense: a body of rules that applied to a definite, bounded domain of social existence. At the end, in our own time, the scope of law has expanded; it has become a gigantic, total presence. The function and meaning of legal process has expanded qualitatively as well as quantitatively. This has blurred the distinction between what is "properly" covered by law and what is not. Spheres of human life, once havens of immunity from law and legal process, were now invaded and (to some degree) conquered.

Another way to describe what happened in modern times is in terms of legal culture; that is, in terms of cycles of demand and response. People came to feel that it was possible to control situations of peril or need—that government inspectors, for example, could make sure canned meat was not rancid or poisonous. This was followed by a concrete demand that the state should exert that control. The government, in response, enacted laws about pure foods and drugs, meat inspection, and the like. These laws changed the legal landscape and set new forces in motion. More important perhaps, they changed the very definition of "legal" in people's minds, changed the level and shape of public expectations, ideas about what was possible, what was natural, what was feasible through law. This in turn encouraged a fresh round of demands. The process spiraled in the direction of more law, more state intervention.

The end result, from the vantage point of 1984, is a radically altered legal culture. Specifically, two new social principles, or superprinciples, appeared as part of American legal culture. Perhaps these are better thought of as two clusters of expectations. The first is what we can call a *general expectation of justice*; the second is a *general expectation of recompense*. The first, in brief, is the citizen's expectation of fair treatment, everywhere and in every circumstance. Justice here is not merely a matter of courtroom procedures. Justice is, or ought to be, available in all settings: in hospitals and prisons, in schools, on the job, in apartment buildings, on the streets, within the family. It is a pervasive expectation of fairness. And it is substantive as well as procedural.

The second general expectation is obviously connected to the first one. It is the general expectation that somebody will pay for any and all calamities that happen to a person, provided only that it is not the victim's "fault," or at least not solely his fault. This is, in a way, only a special case of the first social principle. It is, in part, what people really mean by fairness or justice. Justice is not only fair treatment by other people and by government; it also means getting a fair shake out of life. Life is certainly "unfair" if a man buys a can of soup and dies of food poisoning. If a person is hurt in a tornado, or hit by a car, or born with some terrible defect, these situations, too, can be described as unfair. People even *call* them unfair, even though they know that nobody is really "responsible." They also tend to feel that there ought to be some sort of redress; someone should pay.

The next chapters will flesh out this argument and look at the evidence. Part II will introduce still another concept, legal personality, and connect developments in modal legal personalities to the argument sketched out in Part I.

NOTES

1. For an example, see the treatment of the "rudimentary" law of the Eskimo in E. Adamson Hoebel, *The Law of Primitive Man* (1961), ch. 5.

2. See Richard D. Schwartz and James C. Miller, "Legal Evolution and Societal Complexity," *Am. J. Sociology* 70 (1964):159.

3. See Sidney Fine, *Laissez Faire and the General Welfare State, A Study of Conflict in American Thought, 1865–1901* (1956).

4. This is put forward as a general proposition. There are, of course, "advances" in technology that have raised the opposite possibility—complete loss of control; forces that threaten total chaos and the breakdown of society. The atom bomb is a prime example; pollution of air and water, poisoning of the ozone layer, and depletion of natural resources are others. But these come rather late and recent. They may have powerful long-term effects on popular culture, and hence on legal culture. In the short run they merely reinforce the grip of the state.

4

THE SECURITY STATE

AS WE MENTIONED, the most striking aspect of the modern state is its overwhelming size. Government is big in every dimension: it has the most money income; it spends the most; it has the most people on its payroll. Modern states handle immense amounts of wealth; anywhere from a quarter to a half of the gross national product flows in and out of the coffer of the central government. The national budget of the United States government is something on the order of $800 billion. This is more money than most people can even imagine. By way of contrast, the federal government (which, as noted, spent about $11 million in 1800), spent $500 million in 1900, about $8 billion a year during the height of the New Deal's "reckless" spending spree, about $100 billion in 1962, and $200 billion in 1970.[1]

These dollar figures, of course, do not even begin to suggest the actual role of government, its importance in the daily life of the population. For the millions on government payrolls, state, federal, and local, the government is the boss, the supplier of paychecks. Millions of people are wards of the state, in one way or another—prisoners, members of the military, school children, residents of VA hospitals. Millions receive pensions or other money from the state: old age or disability payments; veterans' benefits; aid to families of dependent children; food stamps; payments for not growing peanuts or corn; student loans, disaster loans, small business loans—the list is almost endless.

The power of the state is immense in other ways. The state runs the criminal justice system. It patrols the highways. Police departments, the army and air force, the National Guard, the FBI—all are part of government; and the government owns tanks, aircraft carriers, and fighter-bombers, not to mention the hydrogen bomb.

The *range* of government activity also seems limitless. One can get a rough idea by leafing through the index of a modern state statute book. Taking Virginia as an example, in its thick volumes we find laws on almost every conceivable subject, from A to Z. The "A's" include such obvious topics as abortion, aviation, arson, and attorneys-at-law; plus such headings as apples (elaborate regulation of commercial apple growing), the applebutter championship contest, assumed names, and artesian wells. One double page, under the letter S, includes entries for skiing, slaughterhouses, slot machines, slugs, slum clearance, Smithfield hams, snakes, and snowmobiles. And so it goes, all the way to zoning, the last entry in the statute book.

Statutory words on a printed page do not necessarily mean dense daily regulation; but at the very least, the Virginia statute book implies a vigorous, richly textured public sector. Where does all this activity come from? And what is it for? At some level, all this law making, all the increase in the scope and power of the state, must come about in response to demands from society itself, or from some organized portion or group within society. "The state" is not a self-contained system; it has to be fed and watered, like a plant. To some degree it is under the control of its public, whether by this we mean the general public or some smaller elite. The state, in the last analysis, developed its characteristic modern form in response to a vast increase in demands and expectations.

Take one example already mentioned: product safety. How did the state get into the business of running programs to regulate food and other products—rules about drugs, meat and vegetables, automobiles, toys? Why is there a federal agency with power and duty to decide whether a company can use some additive to make maraschino cherries redder, or cucumbers greener? Why is Washington concerned with labels on mattresses or products made of wool? Each entry in the statute book has a history, and the history is a history of demands.

The story of meat inspection law, and the first federal food and drug law (1906) is an often-told tale. In the background was Upton Sinclair's novel, *The Jungle*. This masterpiece of muckraking described the miserable lives of workers in Chicago's meat-packing plants; what is more to the point, it accused the packing houses of putting out putrid, rat-infested, moldy meat. A storm of protest overwhelmed the Congress.

National food and drug law, in other words, began as a response to public pressure, which built up around a specific incident or scandal—a frequent pattern. Many food companies resisted regulation; that is, they had their own pattern of demands, and the law, to be sure, reflects this resistance as well as the pressure from the other side.[2] In this case, pressure for regulation was not confined to some particular stratum of society; everybody, rich and poor, is in favor of food regulation. Nobody wants to leave the dinner table poisoned. Scandals and outbursts of public opinion have continued to play a role in the development of food and drug law. In 1938, a sulfa drug killed 107 people; afterwards, Congress amended the Pure Food and Drug Act to forbid the sale of drugs without approval of the Food and Drug Administration.[3]

An uproar over poisoned meat or a drug that killed 107 innocent people is no surprise. This pattern of demands and responses is so natural to us that what seems puzzling is the period *before* FDA, not FDA itself. Let us try to step back into that period in order to understand the source of the demands and how they broke with the past.

If one starts, say, in the early nineteenth century and reconstructs the nature and quality of life, one point is immediately striking: life itself was precarious. It hung by a thread. There was, to begin with, no real defense against plague and disease. Medicine was primitive by modern standards; on the whole, doctors probably killed more people than they helped. Infants, especially, died at a staggering rate.

All this was part of an age-old pattern. As Hobbes said of the state of nature, life was nasty, brutish, and short. Nastiness and uncertainty persisted far beyond the state of nature. Lawrence Stone has graphically described the facts of life in the sixteenth century: the typical man was one of four, five, or six children; two or three of these would surely die before age fifteen. He would marry at twenty-six or twenty-seven, and have four to six children himself; two or three of these too would die young. There was an even chance that he or his wife would die before their middle forties. Women, of course, often died while giving birth.[4]

This was England, some centuries before the beginning of our story. But the presence of death continued to be part of life, everywhere, including this country. Life was uncertain from day to day. Men, women, and children were exposed to sudden, violent catastrophe. Society had, necessarily, a "powerful intimacy with death."[5] And nothing could be done to guard against sudden death, or to ward it off.

In the nineteenth century, people were probably, on the whole, healthier than their ancestors of the sixteenth century. But there was still no way to cure or even deal with most major diseases. (Vaccination for smallpox was a significant exception.) Plagues of cholera and yellow fever claimed thousands of helpless victims; successive cholera epidemics, for example, ravaged New York in the nineteenth century.[6] Children died routinely from childhood diseases. When a child fell seriously ill, parents waited helplessly, hoping the "crisis" would pass.

The uncertainties of bodily life had their counterparts in economic affairs as well. Here too people lived in the shadow of sudden catastrophe. Consider, for example, the facts of life for the average American in the nineteenth century—a person living in one of the world's most prosperous countries. There was of course no such thing as unemployment insurance. There were no pensions, public or private, and no social insurance to speak of. If a man lost his health and his job and had no savings, what could he and his family fall back on? If they were lucky, relatives, friends, or their church might help. There was some private charity, too, but little beyond that. Women were in an even worse position. The death of their breadwinner could plunge them into total destitution.

There was, to be sure, a system of relief, the so-called poor laws. But this form of welfare was, in modern terms, primitive and harsh. Local poor relief was niggardly and minimal. In the early nineteenth century, many states converted to a system of "indoor relief": poorhouses and poor-farms. These would take the poor in and keep them from starving, but in both theory and practice, the poorhouse experience was supposed to be so unpleasant that the needy would "go to great lengths to avoid public support."[7] The poorhouse, then, was an option only for the most desperate, destitute people.

When a worker died of disease or by accident, this was often a catastrophe for his family. There was no workmen's compensation. There was only a remote chance of collecting money from the employer. There was no general expectation of liability. People did not expect compensation from anyone—not the employer, and not the state. In a well-known passage in Mark Twain and Dudley Warner's novel *The Gilded Age*, the authors describe a terrible steamboat disaster. Twenty-two people died, scores were missing or injured. But on investigation, the "verdict" was the "familiar" one, heard "all the days of our lives—'NOBODY TO BLAME.' "[8]

In this passage, Twain and Warner referred to two types of catastrophe: sudden death, and sudden economic disaster. The second was, of course, left implicit. But if there was no liability, if nobody was to blame, what would become of the widows and orphans left behind by the steamboat disaster? Few people—and only the rich—owned any life insurance before the middle of the nineteenth century; there was even a widespread belief that life insurance was immoral.[9] In 1850, there was only $97 million worth of life insurance in force in the United States. This rose to $7.5 billion by 1900, which seems like a great deal, but in 1970, by way of contrast, the amount on the books was $1,402 billion.[10] Life insurance would ultimately make a tremendous difference; but for the vast majority of nineteenth century workers and their families, there was no cushion at all against sudden poverty, as great a danger as sudden death.

The small businessman or merchant was hardly better off. There was no stable banking and currency system in the first part of the century. The credit system depended on private paper and notes issued by banks. Banks had the depressing habit of failing at crucial times. Government insurance for bank deposits was unknown before the 1930s. There was also no Securities and Exchange Commission, and hardly any protection against investment frauds, which were wildly common. The economy was subject to unpredictable cycles of boom and bust; "panics" and "crashes" occurred roughly once a generation. Credit was unutterably precarious. An entrepreneur might struggle for years to build up a business, only to lose it in some economic storm or forfeit everything because a ship sank, or a partner failed, or a bank went under in the night. For that matter, there was not even a national bankruptcy act, except for a few brief periods, before 1898. There were state insolvency laws, which covered some of the problem, but these laws were uneven, chaotic, and often unfair.[11]

Most people, of course, were not merchants; nor, for that matter, were they factory workers throughout most of the nineteenth century. The bulk of the population lived as farmers, farm workers, or members of farm families. This life was in some ways the most precarious of all. There were no crop supports, no parity, no soil bank. One year, crops might be bountiful; the next year they might fail because of wind, frost, disease, drought or locusts. Farmers were also chronic borrowers, and the business cycle was an economic plague for many of them far worse than locusts.

Life, in short, was a drama of tremendous uncertainty. A person could not expect to pass through life without sudden catastrophe—in other words, life was filled with cosmic unfairness, or, if you will, injustice. Edmund Ruffin of Virginia, born in 1794, had eleven children. In a period of a few months, in 1855, he lost three of his grown daughters. In his diary, in 1857, he mused over the prospects of living until the age of eighty: "how many things would probably occur before that time, that would be worse for me than my own death. . . . How many . . . beloved children or grandchildren might I not lose by death . . . if my life were so extended." Ruffin was right: he outlived eight of his eleven children before he committed suicide in 1865.[12]

There is no systematic information about the attitudes of ordinary people toward life and its calamities. Were they bitter over the "injustices" of life, the catastrophes that plagued them and their families? Calamity might be part of God's powerful but secret plan; this was an idea at least as old as the Book of Job. Religion played a central role in the lives of believers; it shaped and affected their outlook on life and their interpretation of the seen and unseen worlds. Its importance in understanding the nineteenth century outlook would be hard to overestimate.

But religion was not a way to avoid calamity; it was a cushion, a consolation, a way to cope and accept, a protection against psychic ruin. Another mode of coping was, and is, the so-called belief in a just world; that is, belief that there *is* cosmic justice. To believe this, people have to adopt various strategies for explaining why the world appears unjust; these strategies include modes of blaming victims or blaming oneself.[13]

It is hard to be sure about the mind of the past. There is no window to peek inside peoples' heads, no survey data, and the written record is hard to interpret. It is unclear how far back in time the "belief in a just world" goes; how willing or unwilling people in past times were to accept misfortune, or what its general impact was on personality and way of life. There was, however, nothing much that could be done to avoid catastrophe. It is plausible to think that the grim facts of human life made a powerful impression on human consciousness. Art and literature certainly reflect themes of danger and death, and there are universal patterns and themes of justice and magic in fairy tales and in fiction that suggest a deep inner longing for a world where right triumphs, where the good receive rewards, where justice is neat and comprehensible. (These themes are, of course, by no means dead.)

The facts of life surely found reflection, too, in legal culture. In life there was no general expectation of justice or fairness; no general expectation that somebody or some agency would provide compensation for material loss. And in the legal system, too, the situation was basically the same: no general expectation of justice, no norms that promised justice in every circumstance, no rules that generally promised compensation. That was reserved for another world.

What has happened since the nineteenth century amounts to a major revolution in legal culture as well as in the social order. Technology has made the world over, and in so doing has vastly reduced certain kinds of uncertainty; it has also opened the door to a vastly greater level of demands on government. Slowly people have come to expect more out of government, out of law, out of life. The mechanisms may be obscure, but one key factor is the sense that there are ways to exert control over many of man's ancient contingencies. Technology is crucial in generating this sense of control. Science and machines can conquer disease, lift the curse of early death, protect against disaster, solve the problems of the world. And from physical control the mind moves, in time, to social, collective control.

At the end of the process, what people come to expect is a higher level of justice—social justice, life justice. Of course, it is always a question of more or less. Life is still grossly "unfair," and perhaps will always be. Auto accidents, sudden illnesses, financial reverses: these still strike like lightning, killing happiness and stability, wreaking havoc on innocent victims, spreading darkness and grief. It is even possible to argue that the general reduction of uncertainty in a society like ours is something of an illusion. After all, millions of people are out of work, more and more children are raised by single parents, and as many families are disrupted by desertion and divorce as were once disrupted by death. Perhaps in many ways, life in sheltered villages centuries ago was less unsettling than modern life in the big city. People were nestled in the womb of a tight social order, warmed by deep religious faith.

But primitive or feudal societies are not the baseline against which I want to measure the changes discussed in this book. That baseline is the world of the Industrial Revolution, which destroyed village life and has been ruthlessly destroying all vestiges of "primitive" society. Whatever one might say about society in the distant past, it seems clear that there have been dramatic, exalted, far-reaching reductions in the uncertainties of life, compared to 1800 or 1850. Life remains, in many regards, precarious. But it is bound to seem less so than before. And what is notably different is the *expectation* of sufferers. They expect some kind of recompense, some attempt to make up for their loss.

The changing legal culture leaves its imprint both on public and on private law. It creates, on the one hand, the welfare state; on the other hand, it works a revolution in such obscure and workaday fields as the law of landlord and tenant, and the law of personal injuries.

Sticks and Stones and Broken Bones: The Law of Torts

The law of torts is that branch of the law that deals with "civil wrongs," as the lawyers put it. Torts are wrongful behaviors that fail to measure up to some standard; and the word "civil" distinguishes a tort from a crime. Crimes are also often torts, or imply a tort (murder and theft certainly do). But the reverse is less often true. All torts are by no means crimes. It is a tort to back your car carelessly into your neighbor's hedge; you may have to pay for the damage, but you will not be arrested, fined, or put in jail.

The law of torts, as lawyers understand it, is a ragbag of miscellaneous wrongs, including trespassing on a neighbor's garden, slandering someone, committing assault and battery or malicious prosecution, and invading the right of privacy. But for all practical purposes, the modern law of torts is the law of personal injury. Probably 90 percent or more of all litigated tort cases fall under this heading—people hurt by automobiles, trains, buses, or heavy machinery; people who slip on the stairs at work or on the sidewalk in front of a store; people who break out in a rash after using a certain brand of cold cream; people who have surgery and end up with a sponge or a scalpel inside them.

Torts is a fairly old branch of law; its common-law roots go back to the middle ages.[14] Of course, legal rules about personal injury are *very* ancient; Hammurabi and the Talmud had no norms that correspond with antitrust law or the corporate income tax, but they certainly had rules about personal injury. Nevertheless, the law of torts did not loom large in the common law before the nineteenth century. Not a single treatise on the subject was published in English before the middle of that century.[15] Nor was an important body of accident law hiding under some other heading. What breathed life into this ancient body was the Industrial Revolution and, especially, the invention of the railroad locomotive. Before the Industrial Revolution, bodily injury from accidents was not much of a social problem. Of course, people fell off roofs or into ditches; they were kicked by horses or bitten by dogs. There were injuries on the road from reckless carriages and horses. But for efficiency in mangling people, en masse, there is nothing like the modern machine. Machines are efficient at doing work, but they are also terribly dangerous. And the railroad was the most dangerous instrument of all.

It was, of course, ancient doctrine that a person could sue for damages if somebody inflicted an injury on him without justification. But only in the nineteenth century did tort law develop an intricate network of rules. There is a good deal of dispute about how this body of law was built up; what rules and concepts came first, and how and why they changed; the precise relationship of tort law to the felt needs of the times, to the desire for economic growth, to legal tradition, and so on.

What is certain is that the law of torts, in the first part of the nineteenth century, grew rapidly, and that it generated rules that put serious obstacles in the way of actions for personal injury. The rules favored defendants over plaintiffs, businesses over individuals. Many of these rules were stark inventions of the nineteenth-century courts. Scholars are not in agreement about what the prior law was like. Some argue that the principle of strict or absolute liability (you do harm, you pay) dominated it.[16] Recently, however, Robert L. Rabin has argued that the old law was dominated instead by the principle of no-liability. Most wrongs did not give rise to any right to payment at all.[17] This view strikes me as persuasive, but in some ways it hardly matters for our purposes which of the two is correct. The social context of the two periods was different. The world of the machine was not the world of manor houses and ancient towns. The laws of torts was bound to undergo drastic change. The new rules, fashioned and refashioned by courts in the crucible of litigation, showed a definite preference for enterprise, for business defendants. They disfavored the potential plaintiffs, who were workers, passengers, pedestrians.

The first and most basic of these rules was the fault principle itself. It was not enough to show that somebody performed an act that injured me; I also had to show that the person was negligent; that is, at fault. Or, to put it another way, I had to show that his conduct did not live up to legal standards, to the standards of the "reasonable man." If he had been careful (according to these lights) and conformed to those standards, I could collect no damages. I would have to bear the loss myself.

The classic expression of this rule is found in a famous case, *Brown* v. *Kendall* (1850).[18] Two dogs were fighting; Kendall took a stick and started beating the dogs, trying to get them apart. With his back to Brown, Kendall raised the stick, "to strike the dogs"; unfortunately, he "accidentally" hit Brown in the eye, and injured him severely. The chief justice of Massachusetts, Lemuel Shaw, wrote the opinion, overturning a judgment for the plaintiff. Kendall was liable only if he fell short of "ordinary" or "due" care; if he had used due care, he would not have to pay, even though he had inflicted an injury on Brown.

Almost as important as the fault principle, perhaps, was the doctine of contributory negligence. If A sued B in tort, and B could show that A had been even slightly careless himself, there would be no recovery. Contributory negligence was a bar to an action for damages.[19] Assumption of risk was another limiting doctrine. Under certain circumstances, a person was supposed to be aware of risks and dangers. He was therefore treated (legally) as if he had voluntarily "assumed" any risks. This often conforms to common sense. If a fan buys a ticket to a ball game, sits in the bleachers, and is hit by a ball, the fan has (or had) no right to sue. Anybody who went to a ball game was supposed to know about this minor risk; spectators more or less agreed to run the risk for themselves.[20] Other instances of the doctrine were not so obviously matters of common experience. In general, the doctrine was an important restriction on the rights of the injured to collect compensation.

Assumption of risk goes back, in this country, to a famous case, *Farwell* v. *Boston and Worcester Rr.* (1842).[21] The case has an even greater claim to fame, however: it is the leading American case on the most notorious nineteenth-century rule of limitation, the fellow-servant rule. The first case on the subject was English, *Priestley* v. *Fowler*,[22] but the doctrine quickly crossed the Atlantic.[23] The opinion in *Farwell* was written by the same Lemuel Shaw who later wrote *Brown* v. *Kendall*. *Farwell*, as the name suggests, was a railroad case. The plaintiff, Nicholas Farwell, worked as an engineer on the railroad. Another railroad worker, a certain Whitcomb, who was a switchman, carelessly left his switch "in a wrong condition." Farwell was on an engine, and was thrown to the ground "with great violence"; the wheels of a car crushed his right hand. He sued the railroad for damages.

Farwell based his case on the maxim, *respondeat superior:* a principal (or employer) is responsible for the acts of his agents and employees. This is a fundamental maxim of the law of agency. Farwell could have sued Whitcomb, of course—the man whose negligence was the actual cause of the accident. But Whitcomb was a railroad worker; almost certainly he had no money to pay damages. In a striking and boldly crafted decision, Shaw turned down Farwell's claim. A "servant" (employee) injured on the job could not sue his employer if the injury was caused by the negligent act of another employee. This came to be known as the fellow-servant rule.

The consequences were plain, and fairly drastic. Carried to its logical extreme, the *Farwell* case meant *no* recovery at all for industrial accidents in factories, railroads, and mines. The principal (the boss) was a distant figure or, more and more often, a mere abstraction—a corporation. Almost necessarily, carelessness that caused accidents was the carelessness of fellow workers. If the Farwells of the world could not sue their employers in case of accident, practically speaking they could sue no one at all.

The fellow-servant rule was politically and economically significant, as one can well imagine. There is something of a literature on its origins, its development, and its meaning.[24] Did the judges know what they were doing when they set this doctrine loose on the world? Some scholars treated the doctrine as a deliberate attempt to subsidize young industry, especially railroads. Shaw, in this view, purposely framed a doctrine that would leave railroads free from the burden of liability. This would encourage the building of railroads and foster the growth of the economy.[25] Other scholars were not convinced. Roscoe Pound, in a famous essay, argued for the primacy of legal doctrine (the "taught tradition") in accounting for the fellow-servant rule. He rejected "economic" theory, as he put it. At any rate, class-consciousness of judges (he said) was not an adequate explanation for the rule.[26]

Pound's argument, essentially, is against trying to apply economic arguments too mechanically; the method cannot be used to account for individual cases. Thus far his point is plausible. But with regard to the fellow-servant rule, the argument is not easy to swallow. This was the period in which a great and dominant value underlay legal policy: it was, in Willard Hurst's phrase, the policy of "release of individual creative energy."[27] This was an era, in short, committed to economic growth. Pretty nearly everybody who mattered in society seemed to accept economic expansion as a general goal. Railroads (like roads, bridges, canals, ferries, and turnpikes) were essential underpinnings for this kind of growth. If the "taught tradition" by accident gave birth to rules which coincided neatly with doctrines people thought of as helpful to economic growth, it would be an amazing coincidence indeed.

No doubt "taught tradition" tended to throw up particular turns of doctrine that flowed rather "naturally" out of past constellations of law. But which of these rules and doctrines survived? The ones that fit the dominant boosterite mentality of the period. This does not mean, of course, that any particular formulation of doctrine was "inevitable" in a strict sense or "determined" in every detail by economic needs; least of all does it mean that the class solidarity of judges shaped them in a conscious way.

But I want to make a somewhat different point here in regard to the fellow-servant rule. A rule of this sort was acceptable in the nineteenth century for a number of reasons. One reason was utility; another was that the rule did not look (as it later did) like a jarring exception to a general theme in the law of torts. Recovery for losses was not the norm in torts; exactly the opposite was true. In this sense, Professor Rabin's point is convincing; and in any event, "no-liability" best describes the tort world of the early nineteenth century. And the tort world was part of a bigger world, legal and social, in which sudden disasters were prone to occur; when they did, nobody except family and friends were likely to come to the rescue with money and help. The fellow-servant rule, in other words, was one more example of the principle of the uncertainty of life and the prevalence of sudden disaster.

This is not to deny the economic thrust of the rule, which was significant. Tort rules that limited liability fit neatly within the fabric of law. The policy of the times was not to impose heavy burdens on enterprise. But at the same time, no-liability rules did not offend norms of general culture. The fellow-servant rule did not seem as heartless to Shaw's generation as it did to later generations. Partly this was because the rule emerged at a time when there was no great industrial work-force—certainly not an organized, class-conscious one. But it is also plausible that the fellow-servant rule did not seem cruel for an additional reason: the legal culture of the time was a culture of low expectations. Recovery for losses was not the norm; hence, the rule seemed neither particularly cruel nor out of place.

Another classic tort case, *Ryan v. New York Central Railroad Co.* (1866), illustrates a similar theme,[28] and exemplifies a key concept of nineteenth- century tort law, proximate cause. This concept requires a close connection between the negligence and the injury: the connection must be "proximate," and not "remote." In *Ryan*, a fire broke out in a railroad woodshed in Syracuse, New York. Ryan owned a house about 130 feet from the woodshed. The fire roared on, apparently out of control, and Ryan's house "took fire from the heat and sparks." In the end it was "entirely consumed."

This too was a case where negligence was not the issue. The railroad had been obviously careless, and carelessness was plainly the cause of plaintiff's misfortune. Yet Ryan lost his case. The stumbling block was the distance between Ryan's house and the place where the fire started. Or to put it another way, what upset the court was the sheer magnitude of the disaster. Suppose the fire had destroyed a whole town—a whole community? Would the railroad still be liable? That might mean the end of the railroad. A principle that imposed liability in these circumstances, then, might bring on "the destruction of all civilized society. No community could long exist, under the operation of such a principle." In a "commercial" country, everybody, "to some extent," runs the "hazard of his neighbor's conduct." Each person, "by insurance against such hazards, is enabled to obtain a reasonable security against loss."[29]

The reference to insurance is striking, and possibly crucial. What seemed to matter was not whether the railroad was at fault, but the economic consequences. The court refused to threaten the railroad with ruin. Thus the case dovetails nicely with others in its tilt toward enterprise. It, too, limited liability. But in *Ryan* the factor of uncertainty seemed to play a crucial part. Business, like the individual, faced enormous, mainly unpredictable, risks. Some risks were too great for any business to bear, fault or no fault. Unless the company could spread the risk, the losses had to lie where they fell. Insurance is one way to spread risks, but under the facts of *Ryan*, and in the nineteenth-century context, individual landowners were better able to protect themselves (by buying fire insurance for their property) than a railroad, which could burn down whole cities at a time.

By the same token, the court does not blink at letting calamity fall on Ryan. The result, in other words, did not seem so cruel and unfair as to make the judges instinctively reject it. After all, other calamities could have struck poor Ryan. Lightning, for example, might have started a fire and burnt down his house as surely as sparks from the railroad. The age was used to calamity, both inside and outside the law.

This is not to deny the element of policy choice in the *Ryan* case. To spare the railroad from calamity, the court let calamity fall on Ryan. Granted. Hence it is right to stress the economic impact (or assumed impact) of tort doctrines. The point is that the court felt forced to make this kind of choice. One side or the other was bound to suffer disaster, unless insurance could spread the risk, which was unlikely at that time. Ryan, the property owner, probably had no insurance, and the railroad was inadequately insured for this level of risk. Nineteenth-century courts were faced with this dilemma time and time again. Calamity was inevitable—for somebody. It was a fact of life. The courts' role was to choose the right victim. Which of two innocents should be sacrificed on the altar of policy?

Nineteenth-century tort law seems callous when compared to the doctrines of today. But it is naive to look at the change as some sort of moral evolution. The key factor is social change, which has profoundly altered the range of choices courts are asked to make. The nineteenth-century cases were "hard," because courts fully expected one party—or society as a whole—to suffer, whatever the court decided. Courts do not feel that way today, because of insurance and, more generally, because of the reduction of uncertainty.[30]

In any event, a revolution overtook the law of torts in the twentieth century. Every aspect of the nineteenth-century structure was fundamentally altered. The fellow-servant rule was totally abolished; in every one of the states, a new system, workmen's compensation, replaced it. "Fault" has been completely eliminated as a principle in work accidents. Contributory negligence and assumption of risk have drastically weakened their hold on tort law. The fault principle is tattered and torn, even in its surviving domain. "Strict liability" (liability without "fault," or at least without requiring proof of negligence) is, for example, the rule in cases of products liability—cases about defective food, automobiles, or power mowers.

This did not happen overnight, of course; and there are dozens of essays and books recounting the how and the why, mostly for the benefit of lawyers who must cope with this subtle, shifting, complicated field of practice. All the experts agree that the expansion of insurance was a crucial factor. Insurance utterly changed the way courts (and litigants) look at liability. Big recoveries are possible, because they know somebody will pay without suffering calamitous loss. Insurance means that courts do not face the dilemma of the *Ryan* case. The calamity is only on one side: the plaintiff's side. Defendant will not pay out of its own pocket, even a deep company pocket. The insurance company will pay.

It is important to realize what this does and does not mean. Edward White has argued that the "central purpose" of nineteenth-century tort law was to "admonish" people who were "blameworthy"; otherwise, the law let losses lie where they fell. Twentieth-century law, on the other hand, has a different central purpose: compensation.[31] Insurance, of course, is the technique for providing compensation, the social invention that makes compensation possible. New tort theories grew up (White argues); these called into existence certain forms of insurance. I think it is far more likely the other way around: it was insurance that helped transform the law of torts. (Or, even more likely, insurance and tort doctrine interacted, feeding and nurturing each other.)

The basic argument is that the history of tort law reveals the working of a subtle form of mutual influence. Barriers against liability eroded in the twentieth century. Recovery became more certain because of insurance and because of such systems as workmen's compensation, which made recovery certain in various situations. As a result, people came to *expect* recovery; they came to expect compensation. An accident, an injury, no longer meant irreparable (financial) calamity. There might be insurance, there may be a lawsuit, there may be some form of social insurance. In other words, someone will pay. Hence there arises a general expectation of compensation.

Jethro Lieberman, looking at the direction doctrine is traveling, has used the phrase "total redress." There is a judicial postulate, he feels, that "no moral society can permit *any injury* to stand unredressed." He connects this to the rise of what he calls a "fiduciary legal order," which focuses on "the individual harmed," and insists that wrongdoers must assume responsibility.[32] Like White, he puts too much stress on the ethical aspects of these norms. But it seems unlikely that the vast expansion of liability comes from an increasingly sharper sense of the immorality of business, doctors, and the whole class of tortfeasors. Nor does this idea explain where the ethic comes from, and why it became so strong.

Changes in tort law march hand in hand with changes in other fields of law, all heading in the same direction: toward a general theory of compensation. There has been a great deal of writing about the transformation of tort law. Most of it, as is usual in legal scholarship, deals with the printed word, and one specific kind of printed word: published appellate cases. The emphasis in the scholarship is on doctrine, on legal theory. Even the research on appellate cases tends to be unsystematic.[33] Research on legal behavior is much skimpier, to say the least. But there is every indication that behavior too has changed over the years, and in significant ways.

One potent indicator is the rise in recent years in the size of tort recoveries. This development has little or nothing to do with shifts in doctrine in themselves; it has a great deal to do with legal culture— with theories of compensation as they function inside the minds of judge and jury. In the nineteenth century, personal injury recoveries tended to be small. Although there is no reliable information about average awards, apparently no case before 1900 awarded a victim more than $50,000 in a personal injury case. Even allowing for inflation, that would be dwarfed today by dozens and dozens of cases.

Things changed in the twentieth century, at first slowly, then rather rapidly. An appellate case in California, decided in 1911, upheld an award of $70,000.[34] This was probably some sort of record; it was a very sizeable award—perhaps equivalent to $750,000 in 1984 dollars. Nobody sneezes at an award of this size; but top awards today are much, much higher—more than ten times as great. For example, a lawsuit against the Ford Motor Company, in California, was settled for over $10,000,000 in February 1983. The victim, James Hasson, suf- fered ghastly injuries when the brakes failed on his car. The jury awarded $11.5 million. The judge reduced the amount to $9.2 mil- lion, and Ford settled for this amount, plus interest (which pushed it over the $10,000,000 mark).[35]

Tort awards of millions of dollars may seem almost commonplace today but, in fact, mega-awards are not nearly as common as people think. The overwhelming majority of tort claims are settled out of court, and for modest amounts.[36] Even claims that reach the courts tend to settle for low recoveries. An elaborate study of Cook County, Illinois (1960–1979), yielded valuable information about damage re- coveries. This was a study of civil cases, most of them tort cases, that actually went to the jury. The median recovery in civil cases hardly changed at all in the twenty-year period. But the average recovery rose sharply, from $34,000 to $71,000 (expressed in 1979 dollars).

What pushed up the average in Cook County, obviously, was not the ordinary case, but the extraordinary one. Increases were immense in the top 10 percent of recovery. Products liability cases were large to begin with ($496,000 was the average award, in this group of cases, in 1960); they rose to $791,000 at the end of the period. Cases of "street hazards" showed an even more dramatic rise; here the average award in the top 10 percent went from $51,000 to $648,000 between 1960 and 1979—a 1,271 percent increase![37]

What are we to make of these figures? Exactly what is going on in the minds of judges and juries? One thing is clear: juries (and judges) now behave differently from their nineteenth-century predecessors in a number of ways. They no longer have much of a sense of limits. The biggest awards, as always, go to people who suffer the most terrible injuries. What has changed is the culture of compensation, the theory of a proper recovery.

By "theory of recovery," I do not mean legal theory, strictly speaking, least of all the words judges use to "instruct" their juries. Of course, legal theory has changed drastically in the twentieth century. There are new concepts of liability; whole categories of cases give rise to claims that would have been thrown out of court a century ago. But this hardly explains the revolution in damage awards. As to damages, legal theory has not changed very much with regard to the elements that judge and jury may properly consider. The behavior of judges and jurors, however, imply a changed sense of what "compensation" means.

Occasionally, a losing defendant tries to overturn a verdict on the grounds that the jury awarded "excessive" damages. This is a fairly desperate argument, and it does not succeed very often, at least on appeal. Some 633 cases, reported between 1880 and 1930, raised this issue on appeal from personal injury verdicts, in the western states whose decisions appear in the *Pacific Reporter*. The argument was successful in only 122 cases. For the same period, 309 such cases appeared in the *Atlantic Reporter* (it mostly covers the New England states); the argument was successful in only 75 cases.

Appeal courts, in other words, have been reluctant to second-guess juries. They reverse a lower court only when the award is "so grossly disproportionate" to what the facts warrant that it "shocks the sense of justice," and sets up "a strong presumption that it is based on prejudice and passion rather than sober judgment."[38] This "test," or something much like it, appears in case after case. But the cases that "shocked" courts in 1900 would sail past appeal courts today. A losing defendant today would not have the slightest hope of getting a verdict reversed for amounts that stretched the law to its limit in 1900.

Legally speaking, various ingredients enter into the calculus of damages for personal injuries. To begin with, there are actual expenses— medical bills, for example. Then there are lost wages, if any. Next is the loss, if any, in future earning power. Last comes that amorphous catch-all, pain and suffering—a category much criticized by commentators, but deeply entrenched in the case-law. It is responsible for a good proportion of the money damages in major cases.[39]

None of these categories are new. Even recovery for pain and suffering has a decent pedigree that goes back more than a century. What is crucial is how legal institutions handle these categories. Courts—and, as far as we can tell, juries—were most comfortable in the nineteenth century with damages they could actually reckon. Whatever the theory, damages in practice were mostly backward-looking: what has plaintiff suffered so far? Courts and juries were less comfortable with the future, with "damages" to be caused by future suffering or from an impaired and injured life.

From the modern standpoint, then, damages in 1850 or 1900 fell short of full compensation. They did not go into the question of a lifetime of suffering, even allowing for a shorter life-span. The search for damages went on under the shadow of an unconscious theory of limits. It is not hard to understand why. Who, after all, would pay for inflated damages? Businesses as a whole were smaller and more precarious than today. The deep pocket was not so deep. Liability insurance was less widespread. Even more important was the prevailing legal culture, linked to the uncertainties mentioned. There was no general theory of compensation, no notion of total justice. These elements were missing from life and, therefore, missing from law.

These unconscious restraints have now vanished. Almost nothing inhibits the jury (and the court) from searching for, computing, and awarding money that comes as close as one can to full compensation. This is an insured society; the jurors carry insurance themselves, and they expect that an insurance company will pay for whatever damages they award. Of course, nothing can really compensate for a lifetime of suffering; nothing can restore a broken body, blinded eyes, ruined expectations. But past juries did not even try. They were not committed, in their own minds, to a theory of total compensation.

WORKMEN'S COMPENSATION

Tort law, then, has been transformed in the twentieth century. Many old rules of restraint were abolished, eroded, or nibbled to death in the courts. Contributory negligence, for example, has fallen victim to a new theory, comparative negligence, which allows a negligent plaintiff to recover so long as he was less careless than defendant. The fellow-servant rule had a more dramatic end: it was abolished in state after state. The process began shortly after 1910. New York and Wisconsin were pioneers and within a decade or so most states did away completely with the fellow-servant rule. A new system, workmen's compensation, replaced it. The last hold-out was Mississippi, which caved in in 1948.[40]

Workmen's compensation was in many ways a new departure. It dispensed almost entirely with the fault principle. Under workmen's compensation law an employee was entitled to recover for work injuries, fault or no fault. Any accident was covered, so long as it arose "out of and in the course of" employment. Negligence was no longer necessary.

Generally speaking, contributory negligence also ceased to be much of a factor. Many early cases dealt with accidents caused by "horse-play" on the job and other examples of poor work discipline. At first, some courts tended to deny recovery; by the 1940s, this trend had been reversed.[41] Now a worker may recover even if he brought the accident on himself by carelessness or downright foolishness. Foolish is hardly the word for a trucker who urinates off the side of a moving truck, falls off the truck, and hurts himself. These were the facts of a Wisconsin case in 1943; the worker recovered.[42] In fact, under some statutes, the only exceptions are injuries that come from "intoxication," or from the worker's "willful intention to injure himself or . . . another."

The words quoted come from a typical workmen's compensation statute, Idaho's law of 1917.[43] Like the others, it abolished the fellow-servant rule, the fault principle, and put in place a system of "sure and certain relief." (The law also—this was part of its compromise nature—cut off the worker's right to sue his employer in tort). Recovery was certain—but also limited. A totally disabled worker became entitled to a weekly payment of 55 percent of his average wages ("but not more than Twelve Dollars nor less than Six Dollars a week"—this was, of course, in 1917 dollars), for a period "not exceeding 400 weeks"; and $6 a week thereafter. A separate formula covered partial disability; there was also a grisly catalogue of specific "prices" for specific injuries. For example, loss of "one hand" was worth 150 weeks of compensation; "total blindness of one eye" was worth 100 weeks; the "great toe with the metatarsal bone thereof" was worth 30 weeks; other toes were worth only 6 weeks apiece.

A long history of struggle lay behind passage of the workmen's compensation laws. By the end of the nineteenth century, the fellow-servant rule had become extremely controversial. Thousands of workers died or were maimed in industrial accidents each year. Only a few recovered damages. Industrial accidents had become, quite understandably, a political issue. Modern machines were dangerous. There was a demand for safety on the job and for greater economic security. The root problem was slaughter and maiming at work and the resulting destitution and suffering of victims and their families. The law, it was hoped, would give companies incentive to make the work place safe and provide economic relief to workers and families when disaster struck.

There were images of the industrial accident that dominated debate and stood uppermost in peoples' minds: the images of huge factories and mills, noisy, dirty, crowded with roaring, whirling machines, all with sharp gears, teeth, blades, and moving parts; steel mills with hellish, boiling fires; plants with vats of acid; deep and dangerous coal mines, plagued with lethal gas and dust; the enormous, deadly power of great locomotives. Industrial accidents of the "classic" type, coming out of these settings, are still important, and they continue, of course, to be covered by the statutes. But workmen's compensation law has also moved far beyond such accidents in the sixty to seventy years since the laws were first passed. In many ways, the law has traveled the same general road as the rest of tort law. Courts—and to some extent the agencies that run compensation programs—have expanded coverage far beyond what the original draftsmen probably had in mind.

The truck driver who fell off his truck is a fair example of this evolution; other cases might strike the reader as even more extreme. In *Louie* v. *Bamboo Gardens*,[44] a 1947 case, the Idaho statute was interpreted (or stretched) to cover the sad case of a busboy in a Chinese restaurant. Tom Louie, the unlucky busboy, was carrying water glasses from the kitchen to the dining room. At exactly that moment a crazed gunman burst into the restaurant, shooting off a .38 caliber revolver. Bullets hit Louie in the chest and lungs. The Idaho court awarded workmen's compensation. Of course, nobody argued that the employer was at fault, and the incident was hardly an "industrial acci-

dent" in the conventional sense. But it was an injury on the job, and
connected (however vaguely) *to* the job. The statute, said the court,
plainly applied.

Cases have gone even further—there has been litigation about employees injured on parking lots or during baseball games at company
picnics; secretaries who twisted their necks at work; clerks who suffered
heart attacks, or epileptic attacks, or hurt themselves in a fit of sneezing
on the job. In *Bletter* v. *Harcourt, Brace & World, Inc.*, the employee,
Robert Bletter, age thirty-three, in "good spirits" because he loved his
job (no Marxist alienation here), did a little dance step in a self-service
elevator, fell, and fractured his thigh. This, too, was compensable.[45]
In another case, a barber developed a hernia on the job, underwent
surgery, developed heart trouble, became despondent, and committed
suicide. An award of compensation was affirmed.[46]

What shines through in these cases is the tendency of courts to
expand the meaning of the statutes. The statutes cover accidents "arising out of and in the course of" employment. Courts have seized on
this language to allow compensation for almost anything that takes
place on or near the job or is connected with the job in some way,
however tenuous. Of course no language in the statutes says so and no
such doctrine is expressed openly by courts. But the trend of the cases
is unmistakable. Nor is this simply an idea of courts alone. Legislatures
have never protested this development, which they could do simply by
amending the laws; in fact they have added wrinkles of their own.[47]

In some ways, the cases seem irrational. Why should Tom Louie get
a weekly check because an insane gunman shot him at work? If the
same thing had happened on his day off, or on the streets, or near
Louie's house in the morning, before work, he would have no claim
against his employer.[48] Why then should the restaurant pay? It in no
sense was morally or factually responsible. To be sure, the courts do
express some sort of rationale for these cases. They ask if the risk of
injury was enhanced in any way by the job. Even for Tom Louie the
answer had to be yes. Crazed gunmen are a (remote) risk of the busboy
business.[49]

But compensation for this sort of risk was hardly the policy behind
the original statute. Whatever that policy was, it hardly fit Tom Louie,
or Robert Bletter, or Karlslyst, the careless truck driver. In none of
these cases was the employer in any way "at fault." It is hard to see how

the money paid to Louie, or Bletter, or Karlslyst, could encourage employers to make the work place safer. What policy, then, is behind the recoveries? The courts talk about "liberal" interpretation of compensation statutes. "Liberal" to what end? and why?

The mystery fades somewhat when these cases are compared with tort law more generally, and with trends in the legal system as a whole, and if one throws in developments in social insurance and welfare law. In all of these, one can see the shadow of a major social norm, the norm of total justice—the general notion that catastrophes of all sorts "earn" compensation for the victims, so long as the victim was not evil enough to deserve the blows of fate. Workmen's compensation law, in short, "stands in" for this more general norm, which does not exist as a concrete legal principle. Developments under workmen's compensation statutes, like tort developments in general, bend toward the norm, like plants bending and growing toward the light. At least from this broader standpoint, the cases are not irrational or out of place.

Another example of the movement of law, however haltingly, toward this norm, is victim compensation, a striking innovation of recent years. The state, of course, punishes criminals at public expense, and criminals are in theory bound to make restitution to their victims. But you can't get blood from a stone, and most victims recover nothing from burglars, armed robbers, rapists, and thieves. They bear their losses themselves, often, to be sure, with the help of insurance. In 1965, however, California began to offer compensation to victims of crime. The statute recited a "public interest" in helping people who suffered loss because of crime and were exposed to "serious financial hardship."[50] The amounts that California pays out under the program are small, and few people collect.[51] But the principle is significant. The idea that the state has a duty to provide for "innocent" victims reflects a new, and powerful norm: the norm of total justice.

SECURITY AND WELFARE

Workmen's compensation is an important step on the road to a welfare state and an important instance of social insurance; but it also replaced parts of the law of torts, a field of "private law." In fact, injuries covered by workmen's compensation fall into two categories, which are at least analytically distinct. First, there are injuries caused by somebody's "negligence"; in these cases, the workman (at least theoretically) had some chance of suing the company. These were classic tort cases, in other words, although the fellow-servant rule and other doctrines were serious barriers to recovery. In other situations, what happened was legally speaking pure "accident." Tom Louie's injury was one example; but hundreds of other incidents on the job occur every day, some trivial, some serious, that are nobody's "fault" under any theory, but give rise to compensation. Workmen's compensation here acts as social insurance, pure and simple.

Social insurance programs are, of course, an outstanding feature of the welfare state, and the welfare state is the characteristic state of the modern West. Americans live in a welfare state, as do the English, the French, the Germans, the Swedes, and so on. Some scholars prefer to speak of the welfare-regulatory state. This hyphenated name points to two outstanding traits of modern government. First, it administers programs that provide some sort of social minimum—unemployment compensation, old-age pensions, family allowances, food stamps, aid to the blind. Second, it is an active, interventionist state that produces and uses an enormous body of rules in order to control the economy, the money supply, modes of competition, the market in various goods, labor relations, and business behavior.

The sheer size of the state, as noted, is one of its prime characteristics. It is big because it tries to do so much. It has its finger in every pot. But the growth of this superstate is not as mysterious as some of its critics seem to think. These critics (and many eager politicians) compare the growth to some sort of cancer—malignant, strange, out of control. The truth is much more prosaic. The state is not an abstract entity, divorced from concrete social forces and institutions. It is a part of society. The state feeds on the wants of its citizens. Mostly, it grows because its public wants it to grow—not as a matter of principle or political theory, but simply because there are demands that center on government, on collective action. There is a demand, not for big government as such, but for dozens of individual programs and agencies. Together these make up the modern Leviathan.

The nineteenth-century state was small and cheap. Its taxing power was pathetic in modern terms; its corps of employees was minuscule. In some ways, there was never a golden age of laissez faire; American government was always relatively active, especially in promoting the social infrastructure—banks, roads, canals, railroads.[52] The concept of a "release of energy" implies as much. American legal theory in some vague way recognized that the public, the community, had "rights" and that the state had authority (and the duty) to act for the common economic good.[53] Yet, when all is said and done, nineteenth-century government can hardly be compared to its modern descendant. On the whole, the legal system of the time fostered and favored private decisions. Some even think the system evolved in such a way as to "diminish" the role of the "public estate."[54] Law and legal theory conceived of public "rights" and state "duties" in niggling, circumscribed ways.

Why was the state so small in the nineteenth century? What kept it from growing larger and doing more? In some ways, it was true that the state was shrinking: it was, for example, not clear at the outset that banks and railroads were destined for private ownership. The government owned roads and bridges: why not railroads, too? In many other countries, of course, railroads eventually ended up as state enterprises. But as the nineteenth century progressed, the private domain seemed to sweep all before it.

One conventional way to look at nineteenth-century government is through the lens of ideology; specifically, the ideology of laissez faire, or the theory of the night-watchman state. The children of Adam Smith really believed in small government. So the argument runs. They *believed* in the invisible hand. But it is easy to exaggerate the role of ideology in shaping the state during this period. There is another way to look at the matter. Perhaps what really controlled the level of demands was a different aspect of legal culture: not ideas about what the state *should* but what it *could* do; about its ability to control events and circumstances.

Even before the eighteenth century, before Adam Smith ever put pen to paper, the "political culture" in this country, it can be argued, was "opposed to publicly instituted change and innovation."[55] Government, according to Hendrik Hartog, tried to avoid spending its own money (it had very little anyway); in general, government was committed "to a policy of externalizing the costs of action,"[56] or, to put it more bluntly, making the public pay for services and improvements directly. There was, to be sure, a long tradition of interference in the market—even crude attempts at wage and price control.[57] But this was not a tradition of responsibility for public health, safety, regulation of business, and the like, not at least in the direct sense of the twentieth century. Indeed, perhaps the theory of laissez faire developed only when it became actually needed to prevent the expansion of government; that is, when the possibility emerged of effective government intervention, on a fairly grand scale, in "private" economic affairs.

The argument here is that people in this country had a low expectation of justice in private affairs. They also expected little from the public sector. These points must not be misunderstood. The generation of George Washington, John Adams, and Thomas Jefferson believed in a just society. They were willing to fight and die for this ideal. The difference lies in the precise conception of justice, and the expectation that flowed from it. In the next chapter I will discuss the nineteenth-century idea of due process, and show how different it was from the contemporary idea. What people expected from government in the age before total justice was a certain level of physical protection, a certain amount of subsidy for the economy (especially in transport and finance), a criminal justice system, a framework of law, a court system, a post office, defense against foreign enemies, and not much else. They got what they asked for, no more and sometimes less.

Increase in knowledge (or what is thought of as knowledge) in medicine, engineering, and economics means an increase in the capacity of human beings to control "natural" forces collectively. Knowledge really is power; but power for whom? For individuals, certainly; but only up to a point. For one thing, no individual can command the knowledge needed to gain power over the natural (and unnatural) world. Knowledge is a collective good, and its power is collective power, that is, power for the state. In an age of science, the state could accomplish more, could control more, than ever before; certainly more than isolated individuals or even groups of individuals could. Hence a lot more was expected from collective action. For example, the development of public health programs is quite obviously linked to advances in the science of medicine.[58] If humanity had not learned how to cure smallpox, diphtheria, measles, and polio, if insulin and penicillin had never been discovered, people would not expect the state to help pay for vaccinations, drugs, and operations, at least for those too poor to afford these on their own—which, in some cases, means most of us.

Technology does not create demand by itself; all it does is make demand possible. The process (in liberal, Western states) goes roughly like this: science discovers a "cure" for some disease. The discovery gives hope to the victims, but it also, for the first time, engenders a social demand. Victims no longer feel that blind fate, or the gods, control their destiny. It may have been bad luck to get the disease, but chance or prayer is no longer the sole key to the outcome. Now there is a life-giving serum, a miracle operation, a treatment. Thus, if the patient dies, this must mean some concrete institutional failure—or some form of injustice. And in a complex society, a modern society, a society of strangers, private arrangements and markets cannot guarantee justice for victims of this disease. Only through law is there leverage, or power, to make the machinery move.

As uncertainties and impossibilities wither away, the public demands more public action. A process is set in motion; the state gets larger, and its size accustoms the public to a level of demands which in turn increases the size and scope of the state. The process goes on all about us every day. Each advance in power over the environment lays the groundwork, and forms the prerequisite, for demands that the power be exercised. There is a constant upward spiral. The more the state does, the more it becomes active and powerful, and the more people come to expect of it. An enormous public sector then comes to seem natural, inevitable. Finally, it turns into habit, or custom; it is what people know, the environment in which they live and breathe.

Meanwhile, reduction of uncertainty in one area of life leads to demand for reduction of uncertainty in others. This lies at the root of the development of the "social" part of the welfare state. Disasters still occur—fires, floods, earthquakes—but now there are programs of disaster relief. People still lose jobs—alas, all too frequently in recent years—but unemployment insurance acts as a cushion. People still have accidents at work, but workmen's compensation provides a floor of benefits. They still grow old and feeble, but pensions guarantee a basic income, and there are special programs (housing for the elderly, and, very notably, medicare) that grant benefits in kind. And so it goes. The welfare state "has been turned into the insurance state" in a "no-risk society."[59] The state has at least learned how to spread certain risks through a system of taxation and welfare. The insurance mentality spills over into the private sector as well—into the law of torts, as we have seen. Indeed, one of the main points of this chapter is the interconnection between the public and private sectors of the American legal system. They reflect the same legal culture; they influence each other's growth.

Whether public or private, these developments, taken together, have radically transformed society—so deeply and fundamentally that people take the changes for granted. As the changes take place, new norms are generated that reflect the altered legal culture. Law responds, unconsciously, to the climate of opinion around it. In particular, it resonates to the claims summed up in the phrase, "the general expectation of justice." New doctrines radiate throughout the legal system and crop up in all sorts of odd legal corners.

Consider, for example, the implicit social principle or norm that can be expressed, rather inelegantly, as follows: there shall be no calamity so great, so overwhelming, that it utterly and irrevocably ruins a person's life. (There is an exception when the person is monstrously evil or criminally at fault—for example, a mass murderer, or a reckless driver who kills a dozen pedestrians.) Of course, there is no such explicit legal principle. But this norm or principle lies underneath the skin of the legal system. It appears in many branches of law and in many forms and disguises.

It underlies, for example, the modern law of bankruptcy. The root concepts of modern bankruptcy law were unknown to the old common law; in the eighteenth century, bankruptcy was a privilege reserved for "merchants," not for the population as a whole. Imprisonment for debt was a feature of American law well into the nineteenth century. The Constitution of the United States gave Congress the power to pass a national bankruptcy law, but Congress exercised its power very fitfully. National bankruptcy laws were enacted from time to time, but quickly repealed. The modern law dates from 1898; the state versions were chaotic and erratic.[60]

Two fundamental ideas are at the core of modern bankruptcy law: fairness to creditors as a class, and a clean slate for the debtor. The debtor does not go to prison or suffer other indignities. He or she can start over again. This notion of a second chance is the moral basis of bankruptcy. A husband and wife accumulate a little capital and open a pizza parlor, which goes broke within a year. Should they be saddled with debt for the rest of their lives? Going broke is enough of a calamity. The bankruptcy law gives them a chance to start over.

But the bankruptcy law is not the only example of second chances imbedded in custom or law. Society, indeed, is structured to allow many kinds of second, third, even fourth chances. Juvenile records are sealed, then wiped out when the juvenile turns eighteen. People who flunk out of school can usually try again; the educational system is, in general, reluctant to close the doors of opportunity. A high school drop-out can reenter school or earn an equivalency diploma. In many states, community colleges will accept anybody who finishes high school; a "late bloomer" can start climbing the ladder. There are no be-all and end-all exams, as there are (for example) in France.

Another implicit principle is what one might call *tenure*: the (legal) protection of long-term relationships. This too is a product of the new legal culture, a corollary of the general expectation of justice. It too crops up in odd legal corners, though never in a systematic way.

One illustration comes from the law of landlord and tenant. In the "good old days," the law (at any rate, formal doctrine) favored the landlord. The landlord, after all, owned the property. His rights were paramount. He alone had the right to choose his tenants, decide on the rent, and set the terms and conditions of the lease (controlled, to be sure, by the market). Once the lease was up, he had a perfect right to get rid of his tenant for any reason, or no reason at all.

Modern law, on the other hand, places sharp limits on landlords' rights, especially those of residential landlords. In some communities, there are rent control ordinances. A landlord cannot discriminate against blacks, or Asians, or against any ethnic or religious group, under state fair housing laws (and with regard to federally financed housing, under Title VIII of the Civil Rights Act of 1968). In some states or cities, a landlord cannot discriminate against families with children.[61] Taken together, these are substantial restrictions on the "freedom" of the landlord.

There is also the doctrine of retaliatory eviction. In *Edwards* v. *Habib*, a tenant in the District of Columbia rented on a month-to-month basis.[62] She complained to the city about sanitary code violations. The landlord gave notice and tried to get rid of her. The court refused to allow the landlord to evict the tenant, in retaliation for blowing the whistle, even though the tenant's lease was up. Even more startling, from the standpoint of the old law, is the frame of mind exhibited by a statute in New Jersey, which allows a landlord to evict only for "good cause"—here, too, even though the lease is up. The statute spells out the meaning of "cause." "Cause" includes, as one would expect, failure to pay the rent, disorderly behavior, or "gross negligence" that causes damage to the premises. Thus the statute is not as extreme as it seems at first blush. But it marks a definite break with the past.[63]

The argument here is that a principle of tenure underlies, or at least supports, some of these changes in the law of landlord and tenant. Of course other factors are also at work. One is the change in the structure of tenancy—in particular, the rise of large corporate landlords. "Tenure" makes sense only when the relationship between landlord and tenant is impersonal, when they are strangers to each other.[64]

The principle of tenure makes its mark on other areas of law and society as well. "Tenure" in the literal sense is the rule in most places for teachers and other civil servants. There is a parallel development in the law of employment contracts. Labor law in general has moved toward greater job protection: employers, like landlords, cannot discriminate in hiring or firing on the basis of race, sex, religion, and even age; union contracts protect seniority; there are "grievance procedures" in factories and within the family of large employers. Recently, too, a striking new doctrine has popped up in the courts in cases arising out of "at-will" employment contracts. "At-will" employment is what most people have, outside of unions, civil service, the army, or college faculties. It is, in a way, not a contract at all; under an "at-will" agreement, the boss can fire you "at will," that is, whenever he wishes, for any reason or no reason.

In a recent series of cases, courts have begun to nibble away at the doctrine that accepted this power as a right of employers and have begun to protect some unprotected workers. This has happened under the umbrella of a number of legal theories.[65] Courts have unconsciously resonated to the newer social norms. They have had to be legally inventive to do so. Thus, some courts have boldly discovered a brand-new tort—bad-faith firing. Others have read into employment contracts an "implied condition" to the effect that the employer will not fire the worker, except for cause. "Implied conditions" come in two sorts. One sort really is implied (that is, the contract does not say so, in so many words, but reasonable people would read it that way). Other conditions are purely imaginary, but the court inserts them in the interests of fairness. The condition under discussion is probably of the imaginary sort.

These legal developments in housing and employment law are indicators of the way judges and legislators think; beyond that, they tell a story about modern legal culture. This is true even where (as in "at-will" cases) the evidence comes from appellate decisions, which are scattered or even freakish. The cases show an unmistakable sensitivity to tenure, that is, to long-term relationships, a sensitivity largely missing in nineteenth-century cases.

Is it too far-fetched to see the same norm at work in *Marvin* v. *Marvin*, the famous "palimony" case?[66] This California decision, of course, was a great hit in the newspapers and on the evening news (it had everything, including celebrities and sex). It also evoked a lot of solemn discussion about the new morality, the contortions of modern family life, and the like. The legal points in the case were in fact quite slippery and technical. But one thing about the case was quite clear: Michele Marvin spent years sharing a life with Lee Marvin, the actor. She claimed a "contract" right to share in his wealth. The court went at least part way in her direction. Whatever legal disguise the decision wore, it had the effect of recognizing an equity, a right, in Michele Marvin, and a right that accrued over time, that is, in accordance with some shadowy norm of tenure.

To sum up the discussion this far: it is possible to trace, over time, the vague, ragged development of certain new legal principles. These are the reflection, sometimes vivid, sometimes dim, of new social norms, which find their way into legal culture. In the actual, working law, these principles do not find complete expression; rather, they generate bits and pieces here and there. These, taken together, imply two superprinciples: the general expectation of justice, and a general expectation of repayment or recompense for loss. The word "general" is used quite loosely; obviously there are many holes and gaps in these "general" expectations, and certainly in the state of the law. Still, there is a tendency, running in a particular direction and leaving tracks and marks all about the system.

The bits and pieces mentioned in the last paragraph were on the side of so-called private law: torts, contracts, family law. The superprinciples are, of course, also part of the bigger picture; that is, the welfare state itself, with its vast, pervasive programs of social insurance. Indeed, a major theme of this book is the connection between the two domains. They feed on each other, support each other, strengthen each other. And this is only natural; the same legal culture is the basis of both.

If further evidence were needed on this point about private expectations, the "freak" cases might be cited once again—the extreme cases that pop up from time to time in case reports or in the press and are taken as symptoms of the national litigation disease. In one instance, mentioned earlier, a man tried to sue a woman who stood him up on a date.[67] I also mentioned a case in which a man threatened to sue his father and mother for malpractice because they raised him so badly (he said) that he became a nervous wreck.[68] Of course nothing came of these cases, legally speaking. If matters of this stripe get to court at all, judges quickly dismiss them. Still, such cases would have been unthinkable a century ago. Nowadays, they are not unthinkable (somebody thought of them, after all). Unthinkability has shrunk drastically over the years.

Critics, of course, cite these cases as examples of wild litigiousness; claims-consciousness gone mad. They strike me somewhat differently. They are stray instances—pathological, perhaps—of a genuine feature of American legal culture: the general expectation of justice. If somebody senses a wrong, she feels that there must be a remedy, somewhere in the system. These examples, then, are chips off a larger, more significant, block: the welfare state itself, and the principle of social insurance, products themselves of changes in social expectation.

There are signs, too, of the dramatic growth of a general process, in government and private institutions, that goes by the name of "due process." Along with the talk about litigiousness goes talk about a "due process revolution" (revolutions are not what they used to be, rhetorically speaking). Without a doubt, amazing changes have taken place here, in law and society. The next chapter takes up this theme.

NOTES

1. *Historical Statistics of the United States*, Vol. II, p. 1114 (1975).

2. Business does not, of course, always resist regulation, for a variety of reasons. See Eugene Bardach and Robert A. Kagan, *Going by the Book, The Problem of Regulatory Unreasonableness* (1982), pp. 9, 18–19.

3. James Harvey Young, "Three Southern Food and Drug Cases," *J. Southern History* 49 (1983):3, 19–30.

4. Lawrence Stone, *The Family, Sex and Marriage in England 1500–1800* (1979), p. 50.

5. Lewis O. Saum, "Death in the Popular Mind of Pre-Civil War America," in C. O. Jackson, ed., *Passing: the Vision of Death in America* (1977), pp. 65, 71.

6. Charles E. Rosenberg, *The Cholera Years, the United States in 1832, 1849, and 1866* (1962).

7. David Rothman, *The Discovery of the Asylum: Social Order and Disorder in the New Republic* (1971), p. 195.

8. Mark Twain and Charles Dudley Warner, *The Gilded Age* (1874), ch. 4, p. 54.

9. Viviana A. R. Zelizer, *Morals and Markets, the Development of Life Insurance in the United States* (1979).

10. *Historical Statistics of the United States*, Vol. II, pp. 1056–1057 (1975).

11. See, in general, Charles Warren, *Bankruptcy in United States History* (1935); Peter J. Coleman, *Debtors and Creditors in America: Insolvency, Imprisonment for Debt, and Bankruptcy, 1607–1900* (1974).

12. William K. Scarborough, ed., *The Diary of Edmund Ruffin*, Vol. I (1972), pp. 109–110, entry for Sept. 26, 1857.

13. See Melvin J. Lerner, *The Belief in a Just World: A Fundamental Delusion* (1980); Zick Rubin and Letitia Anne Peplau, "Who Believes in a Just World?" *J. Social Issues* 31, no.3 (1975):65.

14. Theodore F. T. Plucknett, *A Concise History of the Common Law*, 5th ed. (1956), pp. 459–462.

15. Lawrence M. Friedman, *A History of American Law* (1973), p. 261.

16. See Charles O. Gregory, "Trespass to Negligence to Absolute Liability," *Va. L. Rev.* 37 (1951):359.

17. Robert L. Rabin, "The Historical Development of the Fault Principle: a Reinterpretation," *Georgia Law Review* 15 (1981):925; see also Morton J. Horwitz, *The Transformation of American Law, 1780–1800* (1977), pp. 85–101.

18. Brown v. Kendall, 6 Cush. (60 Mass.) 292 (1850).

19. Wex S. Malone, "The Formative Era of Contributory Negligence," *Ill. L. Rev.* 41 (1946):151.

20. See, for example, Brown v. San Francisco Ball Club, Inc., 99 Cal. App. 2d 484, 222 P. 2d 19 (1950).

21. 45 Mass. 49 (1842).

22. Reported in 3 M. & W. 1 (Exch. 1837).

23. The earliest American case was in fact a South Carolina case, Murray v. South Carolina R.R., 26 So. Car. L. (1 McMul.) 385 (1841), but the *Farwell* case is much more famous.

24. Lawrence M. Friedman, *A History of American Law* (1973), 409 ff.; another economic interpretation is in Morton Horwitz, *The Transformation of American Law, 1780–1860* (1977).

25. Lawrence M. Friedman and Jack Ladinsky, "Social Change and the Law of Industrial Accidents," *Columbia L. Rev.* 67 (1967):50.

26. Roscoe Pound, "The Economic Interpretation and the Law of Torts," *Harvard Law Review* 53 (1940):365; Gary T. Schwartz, "Tort Law and the Economy in Nineteenth-Century America: A Reinterpretation," *Yale L. Journal* 90 (1981):1717 also attacks the "prevailing view" of nineteenth-century tort doctrine "as deliberately structured to accommodate the economic

interests of emerging industry." Schwartz's analyses of appellate cases leads him to feel courts were more "solicitous of victim welfare" (p. 1774) than they are usually given credit for.

27. J. Willard Hurst, *Law and the Conditions of Freedom in the Nineteenth-Century United States*, (1964), p. 7.

28. 35 N. Y. 210 (1866).

29. Ibid., p. 217.

30. In nineteenth-century commercial cases, courts constantly talked about the importance of protecting the expectations of the parties. They stressed how vital it was to guarantee continuity of doctrine in contract law, the law of negotiable instruments, and other branches of commercial law. It was commonplace in the case-law to chatter about how much better it was to have a principle settled one way or another, than to get it right. But the very stress on (legal) certainty and protection of expectations bears witness in a way to the lack of certainty and protection for expectations in the real world; what the courts are saying is that the law should not add risks to what was already an inherently risky situation. And in the twentieth century, in an insurance-oriented, deep-pocket society, this emphasis in the commercial case-law has definitely weakened.

31. G. Edward White, *Tort Law in America: An Intellectual History* (1980), pp. 148–149.

32. Jethro K. Lieberman, *The Litigious Society* (1981), p. 31.

33. A rare exception is Richard Posner, "A Theory of Negligence," *J. Legal Studies* 1 (1972):29; see also Schwartz, "Tort Law and the Economy."

34. Zibbell v. Southern Pacific Rr. Co., 160 Cal. 237, 116 Pac. 513 (1911). Plaintiff, who was twenty-seven, lost his right hand at the wrist, his left arm below the shoulder, and his left foot at the ankle. The jury awarded $100,000; the trial court cut this down to $70,000.

35. *San Francisco Chronicle* (Feb. 19, 1983), p. 5.

36. H. Laurence Ross, *Settled Out of Court: the Social Process of Insurance Claims Adjustments* (1970).

37. Mark A. Peterson and George L. Priest, *The Civil Jury: Trends in Trials and Verdicts, Cook County, Illinois, 1960–1979* (1982), p. 27. Similar results have now been reported for San Francisco, too, in Michael G. Shanley and Mark A. Peterson, *Comparative Justice: Civil Jury Verdicts in San Francisco and Cook Counties, 1959–1980* (1983); see also Marc A. Franklin, Robert H. Chanin and Irving Mark, "Accidents, Money and the Law: A Study of the Economics of Personal Injury," *Columbia L. Rev.* 61 (1961):1; see also, on products liability, E. Bardach and R. Kagan, *Going by the Book*, p. 283.

38. Harrison v. Sutter St. Ry. Co., 116 Cal. 156, 47 P. 1019 (1897). The verdict in this case, for the death of a sixty-nine-year-old man, was $8,000. The trial court granted a new trial, on the grounds that this was an "excessive" amount. The California Supreme Court affirmed the order granting a new trial.

39. See Jeffrey O'Connell and Rita J. Simon, "Payment for Pain and Suffering: Who Wants What, When, and Why?" *Univ. Ill. Law Forum* (1972):1.

40. See, in general, Friedman and Ladinsky, "Social Change and the Law of Industrial Accidents."

41. Samuel B. Horovitz, "Assaults and Horseplay Under Workmen's Compensation Laws," *Ill. L. Rev.* 41 (1946):311.

42. Karlslyst v. Industrial Commission, 243 Wis. 612, 11 N.W. 2d 179 (1943).

43. Laws Idaho 1917, ch. 81, p. 252.

44. 67 Ida. 496, 185 Pac. 2d 712 (1947).

45. 30 App. Div. 2d 601, 290 N.Y.S. 2d 59 (1968).

46. Reinstein v. Mendola, 33 N.Y. 2d 589, 301 N.E. 2d 438 (1973).

47. On the administration of workmen's compensation, see Philippe Nonet, *Administrative Justice: Advocacy and Change in a Government Agency* (1969), especially pp. 170–171 (on extension of liability).

48. He might, of course, collect disability under Social Security, or from some state program.

49. This is why it was important for the court to stress that the gunman had nothing against Tom Louie personally. In a case from the 1930s, a jealous husband shot a milkman who was

delivering something more than milk to the wife. Compensation was denied. Bluegrass Pasture-land Dairy v. Meeker, 268 Ky. 722, 105 S.W.2d 611 (1937).

50. Cal. Gov't Code, sec. 13959. A parallel provision provides money for "private citizens" injured or killed trying to prevent a crime or catch a criminal, helping a "peace officer," or rescuing a person in danger. Cal. Gov't Code, sec. 13970.

51. In 1971–1972, 173 claims were granted, 254 denied; the average award was only $2,218. "Rehabilitation of the Victims of Crime: An Overview," UCLA L. Rev. 21 (1973):317, 368.

52. See, for example, Harry N. Scheiber, Ohio Canal Era: A Case Study of Government and the Economy, 1820–1861 (1968).

53. See Harry N. Scheiber, "Public Rights and the Rule of Law in American Legal History," Calif. L. Rev., 72 (1984):217.

54. See George Dargo, Law in the New Republic, Private Law and the Public Estate (1983), pp. 1–5.

55. Hendrik Hartog, Public Property and Private Power: the Corporation of the City of New York in American Law, 1730–1870 (1983), p. 66.

56. Ibid., p. 65.

57. See Richard B. Morris, Government and Labor in Early America (1946), pp.18–21.

58. See Barbara G. Rosenkrantz, Public Health and the State: Changing Views in Massachusetts, 1842–1936 (1972). To be sure, the statement in the text glosses over what is actually a long, complicated history. The germ theory and increased understanding of the nature of infection ultimately paved the way for a vast expansion of the sector of public health; in the short run, however, it had some tendencies that worked in precisely the opposite effect. So long as people believed that "filth" caused disease, the remedy was public sanitation; but if diseases were actually transmitted by human carriers, then the remedy was to find, diagnose, and cure these individuals—a classic function of private doctors. See Paul Starr, The Social Transformation of American Medicine (1982), p. 181.

59. Yair Aharoni, The No-Risk Society (1981), p. 1. The result, as far as Aharoni is concerned, is a mess; but of course not everyone would agree.

60. On the history of bankruptcy, see Charles Warren, Bankruptcy in United States History (1935); on state insolvency laws, see Peter J. Coleman, Debtors and Creditors in America: Insolvency, Imprisonment for Debt, and Bankruptcy, 1607–1900 (1974).

61. See, for example, Ill. Rev. Stats. ch. 68, section 3–104; Marina Point, Ltd., v. Wolfson, 30 Cal. 3d 721, 640 P. 2d 115 (1982).

62. 397 F.2d 687 (D.C. Cir. 1968). Skelly Wright wrote the opinion; one judge dissented.

63. See, in general, Mary Ann Glendon, "The Transformation of American Landlord-Tenant Law," Boston College L. Rev. 23 (1982):503; Edward H. Rabin, "The Revolution in Residential Landlord-Tenant Law: Causes and Consequences," Cornell Law Review 69 (1984):517; the New Jersey Statute is N.J. Stat. Ann. sec. 2A:18-61.1

64. See Lawrence M. Friedman, "Comments on Edward H. Rabin, The Revolution in Residential Landlord-Tenant Law: Causes and Consequences," Cornell Law Review, 69 (1984):585; on the interesting developments in British law, see David Nelken, The Limits of the Legal Process (1983)

65. See, for example, L. Steven Platt, "Rethinking the Right of Employers to Terminate At-Will Employees," John Marshall L. Rev. 15 (1982):633; Donald H. J. Hermann and Yvonne S. Sor, "Property Rights in One's Job: The Case for Limiting Employment-at-Will," Ariz. Law Rev. 24 (1982):763.

66. 18 Cal. 3d 660, 557 P.2d 106 (1976).

67. Washington Post (August 18, 1980), p. 1, col. 2.

68. New York Times (June 16, 1980), p. 16, col. 2.

5

THE DUE PROCESS
REVOLUTION

IT IS HARD TO GIVE an exact definition of the legal changes that go under the general phrase, the "due process revolution." They consist at least in part of a vast expansion of procedural rights. "Due process" is, of course, a fundamental constitutional principle. The phrase appears in the Fifth Amendment, and also in the Fourteenth. No one can be deprived of "life, liberty, or property" without "due process of law." "Due process," then, is a technical term of law, whatever else it may mean. The most famous cases about due process are constitutional cases in the Supreme Court. Thus the due process revolution grows out of a specific tradition, the American constitutional experience.

But this point should not be exaggerated. Courts have stretched the meaning of the words "due process" like taffy; they have gone even further with another constitutional phrase, also in the Fourteenth Amendment, "equal protection of the laws." Still, due process (and equal protection) are not matters of words. The text of the Constitution is notoriously sluggish; it barely changes over the years, and the crucial texts (the Fourteenth Amendment, for example) have not changed at all for over a century. The "due process revolution" is therefore the product of social change. Specifically (as I have argued), it reflects a pattern of increased demands on the legal system, a legal culture that interacts with a specific structure and tradition and grew out of changes in general and political culture.

The concept of due process has now been stretched to cover a lot of territory. Fair procedures must prevail in all sorts of settings. To begin with, there are governmental settings. Government, especially administrative agencies, cannot take major actions—actions that affect people's lives—without attention to process. Decisions to drop somebody from Social Security rolls, or to deport an alien, or to zone a neighborhood to keep out businesses or apartment houses, have to conform to complex doctrines that define fair procedures. Also, and very significantly, the concept now covers actions by institutions once more or less immune. It has spread to private institutions. A due process requirement now blankets hospitals, prisons, factories, department stores, and schools. (In this list, I have deliberately mixed together "public" and "private" institutions).

Due process may thus be evolving in the direction of still another superprinciple: no organization or institution of any size should be able to impair somebody's vital interests ("life, liberty . . . property") without granting certain procedural rights. What these rights are is the subject of an enormous body of case law, not easily summed up in a simple formula. They include the right to some sort of notice, the right to argue against what is proposed to be done, and (if the action is wrong or illegal) a fair shake at getting it reversed.

The Fifth Amendment to the Constitution, in which the phrase "due process" appears, was ratified in 1791, which means that, constitutionally speaking, due process is a few years short of its two-hundredth birthday. The idea itself is even older. Its meaning in the legal system has changed dramatically over time. In the nineteenth century, it referred basically to the conduct of criminal trials. Due process meant those steps and procedures that made a trial just and fair. (This meaning is certainly not dead; indeed, the decisions of the Warren Court have infused it with new vigor.) Criminal procedure was important to the revolutionary generation. It had pride of place in the Bill of Rights. Yet criminal process was not, in general, a major issue in the nineteenth century, with some exceptions and aberrations. That is, once the ties with England had been snapped, and the power of the executive tamed, the issue fell back into relative obscurity.

Essentially, nineteenth-century criminal trials were run in a decent manner (at least compared to most societies), even though many things went on that civil libertarians today would find grossly offensive. Rights of criminal defendants were, in general, not at the top of national and state agendas. Constitutions, state and federal, duly listed procedural safeguards: privileges against self-incrimination, rules against unreasonable searches and seizures, against double jeopardy, rights to bail and habeas corpus, and so on. In a rough and ready way, trials conformed to the general constitutional plan. Nothing remotely like the horrors of Nazi Germany or the lawlessness of Latin American oligarchies went on in American courts.

There were, of course, egregious exceptions, especially for such outcast groups as Southern slaves; and police brutality was, to a degree, accepted fact in the late nineteenth century. Even in regard to these deviations, there was little recourse to courts or legislatures. Litigation on the rights of criminal defendants was comparatively rare. A study of criminal justice in Alameda County, California, between 1870 and 1910 found that people accused of crime rarely used arguments about constitutional rights in defending themselves—not even on appeal to higher courts. Nor were federal courts very active on this score, except in a few landmark cases.[1] Before the Fourteenth Amendment was adopted, the federal Bill of Rights did not even apply to state courts, under the doctrine of *Barron v. Baltimore*, decided in 1833.[2] The states, to be sure, had their own bills of rights, but there was no enforceable national standard.

Concepts of due process were relevant in civil cases too. Government could not, for example, seize someone's property, without going through some sort of regular procedure, and without paying for what it took. (This was expressly stated in the Fifth Amendment.) In civil cases, too, there has been radical growth and change in legal consciousness over the past generation or so. Even more fundamentally, the notion of due process has spilled over from the courtroom, to institutional and administrative behavior in general.

A few telling incidents show the evolution at work. *U.S. v. Ju Toy*[3] was an immigration case decided by the Supreme Court in 1905. At that time, Chinese were not eligible under the law to become citizens—a blatantly racist provision. A Chinese born in this country was, however, automatically a citizen, under the Fourteenth Amendment. Ju Toy had lived in China, but he claimed he was a citizen by birth. He sailed to the United States on the steamship Doric. The collector of the Port of San Francisco, an official with immigration authority, disbelieved Ju Toy, and refused to let him land. Ju Toy protested, and insisted on his rights. The Secretary of Commerce and Labor affirmed the Collector's decision.

Now the question was, did Ju Toy have any further rights? Could he claim some sort of hearing in a federal court? The district court thought so; indeed, the court went so far as to uphold Ju Toy's claim to citizenship. But the Supreme Court reversed. "Due process" did not require "judicial trial" in this case. Congress had the power, if it wished, to give an "executive officer" complete authority to decide who could enter the country. The decision of the port official was due process. That was that.[4]

From the vantage point of 1985, *Ju Toy* is an outrage. The immigration law was racist to the core, and the incident violated what would now be considered the most elementary requirements of due process. But *Ju Toy* was by no means exceptional. The famous Brownsville episode illustrates the same frame of mind. A shooting took place near Brownsville, Texas, in August 1906. One man, Frank Natus, was killed; a police lieutenant was wounded. Community suspicion (heavily laced with race-prejudice) pointed the finger of suspicion at a company of black soldiers stationed at Fort Brown, just outside town. Nobody had any idea *which* black soldiers were guilty (most likely all were innocent); none of the soldiers confessed or informed on others. As punishment, the troop was drummed out of the army, a decision made or confirmed all the way up to the commander-in-chief, President Theodore Roosevelt.[5] Here, too, the courts did nothing. One black soldier, Oscar W. Reid, tried his luck in federal court, but he lost at every level of the pyramid. The Supreme Court upheld the executive branch. Whether to discharge somebody from the army, and with what kind of discharge, was a matter within the president's discretion.[6]

These cases show what is (from the modern standpoint) extraordinary deference to administrative authority. Executive power seemed to mean some sort of sanctuary from due process, some sort of zone of immunity. There was a similar attitude toward other forms of authority. Those who ran prisons, schools, hospitals, factories—institutions, public or private—enjoyed a similar kind of immunity. This was not a period that talked much about "rights" that are commonplace today: rights of prisoners, or gay people, or the handicapped, or people in nursing homes, or the retarded, or women, or minorities.

The rise of "students' rights" can serve as an example of the way thinking about rights has been transformed.[7] Little or nothing is heard of such a notion in the nineteenth century. Only a handful of reported cases touched on the subject at all before 1900. These sporadic cases do not show much sympathy for students or parents who complained about rules in the schools. In one Pennsylvania case, a district hired nuns to teach public school. The sisters taught while wearing religious dress, including crucifixes. The court sustained the practice.[8] In another case, in Vermont, 150 Catholic schoolchildren were expelled for missing school to attend services on a Catholic holiday. Here, too, school decisions were upheld.[9]

What the two cases have in common is deference to officials. The schools were like prisons, or the United States Army—or, for that matter, the ordinary factory or shop. That is, these institutions were basically beyond the reach of due process. Not totally, of course: a teacher was not allowed to beat children mercilessly (only moderate "correction" was acceptable), and in a few cases, teachers were punished for going too far.[10] Even prisoners were (in theory) entitled to a level of basic decency. But within broad limits, the teacher's word, the warden's word, the boss's word, was law.

In the discussion of the Brownsville affair, the expression "zones of immunity" was used; scholars talk about the "erosion" of these zones as liability expands and due process takes over more and more territory.[11] But in some ways, "zone of immunity" is a misleading phrase. It seems to imply that these zones—the army, the schoolhouse—were exceptions to some general social or legal rule. The point is exactly the opposite. Due process, as understood today, was the exception. The zones of immunity, as it were, made up the rule.

The last generation or so has turned the matter inside out. The chronology is complex; a full account of the rise of due process would show many baffling twists and turns. But a few landmarks should be mentioned. On student rights, there was the famous *Tinker* case, decided in 1969.[12] The war in Vietnam was raging, and opposition to the war was growing. In this case, some high school students wore black armbands to school as a symbol of their distaste for the war. They were asked to take the armbands off; Tinker and some others refused. The school suspended them and sent them home. Out of this incident arose a court case that climbed all the way to the Supreme Court itself.

That Court upheld the students' rights. School officials, of course, had "authority"; they had the right to keep order, to use discipline. But schools also had to respect the rights of students, including freedom of speech. Students, said the court, do not "shed their constitutional rights . . . at the schoolhouse gate." This is the most famous, often-quoted line from the decision. It seems obvious and trite. But, in fact, it embodies a startling change of direction. In the nineteenth century, rights *were* shed at the schoolhouse gate. Rights were shed at the gates of most institutions in society. [13]

One by one, courts and legislatures have stripped institutions of their former immunity. The army still has vast power over its soldiers, but there have been major reforms in military justice. It resembles civilian justice now far more than in the past. The Brownsville episode would be impossible today. The army, of course, is no longer segregated. In addition, no commander, not even the president, can discharge a soldier without proof of wrongdoing, a hearing, or trial. The country now looks back on Brownsville with shame. The government has admitted its wrong; in 1972, the records of the Brownsville soldiers were officially cleared, and Congress voted a money grant to any soldier who might still be alive. (There was only one: Dorsey Willis, eighty-seven years old.) [14] Theodore Roosevelt would be dumbfounded at this outburst of guilt.

The change in military justice is only one of many examples of a new legal attitude toward authority and due process. Much of the vast field of labor law concerns limits on employers' rights. A boss cannot fire workers merely because they join a union, or complain about work conditions, or because they are handicapped, or black, or over forty, or because he may not like the way they part their hair. An employer can be forced to bargain collectively. The National Labor Relations Board monitors union elections. Employers must comply with state and federal labor standards. Of course, labor law has its own special, complex history, but the movement toward legalization, and the spread of due process run strikingly parallel to developments elsewhere in society.

The law of prisoners' rights forms in some ways an even more startling contrast with the past. This is a new and expanding field that occupies what was once almost a total void. The prisoner, in the nineteenth-century view, had only minimal rights. A guard could not (legally) beat him to a bloody pulp, no more than a teacher could (legally) pass the invisible line that separated sadism from "correction." But prisoners were even less likely to complain than schoolchildren, or parents of schoolchildren; and despite these "rights," prison brutality, especially in the South, and especially against black prisoners, was a national scandal. Even in theory, the Bill of Rights as such did not apply to prisoners. Such rights belonged to "a society of freemen," not to "convicted felons and men civilly dead." The quotation is from a well-known Virginia case, decided in 1871; the judge, Joseph Christian, went on to say that prisoners were "slaves of the State." The convict "has, as a consequence of his crime, not only forfeited his liberty, but all his personal rights except those which the law in its humanity accords to him."[15]

The judicial attitude toward prisoners is well illustrated by a case from a Pennsylvania lower court, decided in 1912. This was one of the rare situations in which a prisoner tried to stick up for his rights.[16] The plaintiff was a prisoner in the Allegheny county jail. There was a chapel in the jail. Plaintiff attended for a while, but then refused to go. The keeper "ordered" him to take part in religious services; when the prisoner refused, he "was punished by being put in the dungeon." Later, the deputy warden "pushed him out of his cell and compelled him to attend . . . religious exercises." This, said the prisoner, denied him his "constitutional freedom of conscience."

In 1985, the outcome of such a case would be a foregone conclusion; it would be unthinkable to force religion down a prisoner's throat. Not so in 1912. The Bill of Rights, said the court, had nothing to do with the case; it did not "apply to compulsion exercised by one person over another," unless the compulsion was "authorized by law." Apparently, this was not the situation in the case before the court. If a member of the "Ancient Order of Hibernians should by force or threats compel an Orangeman to hear mass," this would not violate the Bill of Rights; nor would it be "an infringement for a parent to compel his child to go to church, even though the child may not consent." The court also brushed off the prisoner's claim of "assault" on his person; the jailer had a right to "control" the conduct of prisoners.[17]

Here the court did not even see prison as part of government, bound by the Bill of Rights. Rather, the court looked at a jailer's authority as if it were the same as purely private behavior or a parent's power over children, which in 1912 was almost unlimited. The prison, in short, was a zone of immunity, and a broad zone at that.

But by the early 1960s, the courts began to abandon their hands-off attitude. By 1974, the Supreme Court had decided several cases on prisoners' rights, and it was saying, in a matter-of-fact way, that federal courts should "protect" prisoners against regulations or practices that offended "fundamental constitutional" guarantees.[18] This, like the language of the *Tinker* case, sounds perfectly banal, but, in the light of the past, it was a new departure indeed. Courts have struck down rules denying prisoners access to law books, or limiting the rights of inmates to keep legal documents and papers; they have forced prisons to recognize the religious rights of Black Muslims; they have declared whole prison systems unconstitutional because they were badly or harshly run. Behind these cases, of course, is the ferment of a social movement;[19] but the courts have been for their part quite receptive.

Students' rights and prisoners' rights are only two examples of the work of the "due process revolution." The civil rights movement also is part of this development. A gigantic structure has been erected on the basis of the laws against race and sex discrimination. *Brown* v. *Board of Education* (1954)[20] was the starting point in some ways, though it itself was the product of a long and tortuous development. Then came the great Civil Rights Acts, a decade later. Race-discrimination law powerfully influenced sex-discrimination law, and the movement for racial equality no doubt had an impact on the feminist movement. Both in turn have had a deep impact on the rights-consciousness, and the strategies, of other groups.

Thus more and more is heard about the rights of mental patients, the elderly, the young—just about everybody. In 1967, for example, Congress passed the Age Discrimination in Employment Act. It protected workers who were over forty and under sixty-five from "discrimination" in hiring, firing, and conditions at work. The protected age was later raised to seventy. Most states have their own laws against age discrimination, and some states have gone even further than the federal government. In California, for example, there is no upper limit at all; mandatory retirement has been abolished for all but a handful of workers.[21] Special rights for the handicapped are the product of another recent and startling development.[22] The new rights all have limits, to be sure; many do not work out in practice the way they were designed. But there is no question that the structure of rights is radically different from the structure in the days of *U.S.* v. *Ju Toy*, or the Brownsville raid.

Procedural due process has revolutionized the inner life of private institutions as well as public ones. Stanford University, for example, now has a staggering battery of "procedures" to cover disputes and grievances that arise inside the university. There are grievance procedures for students, for faculty, for staff. There are procedures for disputes over hiring and firing, over tenure, over student discipline. The university has perhaps a dozen different types of process, for different kinds of grievance, at the university level; no doubt there are others at the level of individual schools (such as the School of Medicine, or the Business School), or even at the level of departments.

The procedures can be highly formal. The Stanford Judicial Council, for example, has jurisdiction over all student disciplinary cases.[23] The student has a right to a written notice. SJC will arrange for a hearing, run by an outside lawyer. (She cannot be a member of the Stanford faculty or staff.) This lawyer acts as the hearing officer. At the hearing, the complainant must "establish" his facts "beyond a reasonable doubt." Both sides have a right to counsel.[24]

Of course, many of the formal procedures on the books at Stanford are not used very much. If a student, for example, believes he was unfairly graded, he has the right to appeal the professor's grade. Not one grade in a million is in fact formally reviewed (as opposed to informal wheedling in the office). Does this mean the procedure is a dead letter? Not entirely. In the first place, it *has* been used. In the second place, the mere fact that the procedure is possible signals that no decision is, or ought to be, beyond the reach of fair process.

Stanford University is not a deviant case. The expansion of process, the very idea of process, is much more general. There is a great movement in the direction of the superprinciple mentioned at the start of this chapter. But due process, as it spreads through society, is only one more example of the way in which the basic norms of modern legal culture have been spreading throughout society. It is an offshoot of the general expectation of justice, both in the public and the private spheres. Indeed, most people do not distinguish very clearly between the two. As far as big institutions are concerned, it is hard to tell where the public begins and the private ends. The same is true of felt injustice. It hardly matters to a person whether unfairness comes from the Department of Motor Vehicles, or Sears, Roebuck and Company—or even from an "act of God."

The due process revolution would be impossible unless students, racial minorities, convicted criminals, mental patients and their proxies, and many others, were willing to press their claims. Hence the (real or apparent) decay of *authority* seems to be a crucial feature—the decline in deference to parents, teachers, the state, bosses, the army, and so on. After all, the revolution consists essentially of attacks on authority, or resistance to authority, plus the ground rules for carrying on attack or defense.

The decline in authority seems real enough, although it is hard to prove it with facts and figures over any significant time period. The most that can be documented is a decline in trust in the 1960s and 1970s; that is, in the propensity to believe and follow what authority says.[25] People continue to be quite suspicious of authority, although things may be looking up a bit for authority in very recent times. A poll in 1983 showed trust in government "edging up" for the first time in twenty years.[26] There have always been rebels, of course, and always a few people willing to fight hard for their rights—after all, Ju Toy did appeal, and there was opposition to the cashiering of the blacks after Brownsville—but these few were smothered by the sheer power of authority and its supporting ideology.

The decay of deference and trust is no doubt a complex phenomenon. Attitudes toward authority are in their own way symptoms of other kinds of social change, changes in social relationships. That is, it is wrong to assume a simple change in a simple phenomenon called "authority." Authority itself has changed. Take, for example, the "explosion" in medical malpractice suits. Such cases were quite rare in the nineteenth century, both on the trial and the appellate level (only three cases on the subject were reported in California before 1900). They became more common only recently. In Cook County, Illinois (Chicago is the main city), there were 60 malpractice trials in the years 1960–1964, and 142 in 1975–1979, an increase of 237 percent.[27] Almost all of these were probably medical malpractice cases.

These may not seem like staggering numbers, but they are the tip of
the iceberg of complaints against doctors, dentists, nurses, and hospitals. The "explosion" in malpractice cases was real enough to send
insurance premiums soaring and drive the medical profession into
something close to panic. In 1975, the governor of California, Edmund G. Brown, Jr., declared that the state faced a crisis. Insurance
costs had "risen to levels which many physicians and surgeons find
intolerable"; the very "health of the people" was in danger as a consequence.[28] As a result, the state enacted a package of "reforms," including limits on lawyers' contingent fees.[29]

What brought on this crisis and "explosion?" One explanation runs
as follows: people did not, and do not, sue the old family doctor. This
is at least one reason why malpractice cases were rare in the past. Most
people no longer have a family doctor; relationships with doctors are
fragmented, impersonal. Medicine is incomparably more "scientific"
than it was in the 1800s, and much more highly specialized. Patients
feel themselves handed over from one specialist to another. The result
may be good care for their bodies, but the patients lack a certain solid
confidence in their doctors. There is, according to some observers, a
loss of loyalty, commitment, and trust.[30]

This, then, is another reflex of the dependence on strangers. The
doctor is still an authority, but his relationship to patients is not what it
was. He has moved out of the circle of the primary group; he is now (in
many instances) a stranger. This is almost certainly true if the patient
has to undergo some complicated, sophisticated procedure in a great
urban hospital. Malpractice cases are overwhelmingly likely to come
out of this sort of situation. The process of estrangement (if one can
call it that) is quite general in society. The teacher, too, is more likely
to be a stranger to parents than teachers in the little red schoolhouse; or
if the teacher is no stranger, then certainly the principal is, as are
members of the Board of Education, and so on.[31]

Modern litigation is peculiarly likely to arise out of situations of
estrangement. The word "malpractice" refers primarily to *medical*
malpractice, the most common type; but there is also lawyer malpractice, accountants' malpractice, even teachers' and preachers' malpractice. In each case, the relationship with patients, clients, students, or
parishoners has tended to become somewhat cooler, more impersonal,

bureaucratized, estranged. The emotional distance from doctors, teachers, merchants, and the like, strips away inhibitions against using formal law, just as face-to-face relationships tend, on the whole, to *create* this kind of inhibition. There is also a breakdown of relationships *within* professional communities; doctors at one time were extremely loath to testify against fellow doctors. This is much less true today. The decline of loyalty within the profession is another aspect of a general estrangement.

So much about the malpractice "explosion" is fairly obvious. But there is another point worth making. Malpractice cases come up from the new legal culture. People expect more from their doctors. They are less likely to shrug their shoulders, less likely to accept mistake and failure in medical procedures. The citizen of the 1980s does not expect calamity. Illness may be inevitable, but patients expect to be cured; medical science is expected to solve all but a few intractable problems. When something goes wrong, it is easy to blame doctors or hospitals. *Somebody* must have been careless, or followed the wrong procedures. Otherwise, why did the calamity happen? To use a phrase borrowed from tort law, the thing "speaks for itself."

In any event, it is expected that somebody will pay—that somebody is "responsible." This word, "responsible," has, indeed, a double meaning. I am "responsible" for an act if I did something to bring it about. I am also "responsible" if I am charged with the consequences, whether I was the "cause" or not. Modern legal culture hopelessly confuses these two senses of the word. What is clear is that somebody is, or ought to be, responsible—for a failed operation, for pain and suffering, for losses incurred. Somebody has to pay.

To be sure, malpractice cases have nothing formally to do with the due process explosion. Malpractice is part of the law of torts, a branch of private law. Discussion here, again, oscillates between public and private law. This is precisely the point. The boundaries between private law and the public sector have melted away. Modern legal culture insists on a single, unified domain of fairness and legality and demands a single standard of justice. To satisfy this demand, every institution has to fall into line. Suing doctors and insisting on fairness from the Social Security Administration are two sides of the same great polygon, the same great urge for total justice.[32]

NOTES

1. Lawrence M. Friedman and Robert V. Percival, *The Roots of Justice: Crime and Punishment in Alameda County, California, 1870–1910* (1981), pp. 283–284, 285–286.

2. 7 Pet. 243 (1833).

3. 198 U.S. 253 (1905). Congress had passed laws excluding Chinese laborers and prohibiting Chinese from becoming citizens; see 22 Stat. 126 (Act of May 6, 1882).

4. Justice Brewer dissented vigorously, calling the decision "appalling," and a plain violation of due process. 198 U.S. at 168–169.

5. The incident is described in Ann J. Lane, *The Brownsville Affair, National Crisis and Black Reaction* (1971), and John Weaver, *The Brownsville Raid: The Story of America's Black Dreyfus Affair* (1970).

6. Reid v. U.S., 211 U.S. 529 (1908).

7. See Lawrence M. Friedman, "Limited Monarchy: The Rise and Fall of Student Rights," in *School Days, Rule Days* (in press, 1985).

8. Hysong v. School District, 164 Pa. 629, 30 Atl. 482 (1894).

9. Ferriter v. Tyler, 48 Vt. 444 (1876).

10. See, for example, Anderson v. State, 40 Tenn. (Head 3) 348, (1859); Whitely v. State, 33 Tex. Cr. R. 172, 25 S.W. 1072 (1984).

11. See, for example, Jethro Lieberman, *The Litigious Society* (1981), ch. 6.

12. Tinker v. Des Moines Indpt. Community School District, 393 U.S. 503 (1969).

13. Another landmark case was Goss v. Lopez, 419 U.S. 565 (1975); this case established certain due process rights for students who faced suspension because they had violated rules of discipline. See David L. Kirp, "Proceduralism and Bureaucracy: Due Process in the School Setting," *Stan. L. Rev.* 28 (1976):841.

14. *New York Times* (June 15, 1973), p. 31.

15. Ruffin v. Commonwealth, 62 Va. (21 Gratt.) 790, 796 (1871).

16. Merrick v. Lewis, 22 Pa. Dist. 55 (1912).

17. Ibid., p. 56.

18. Procunier v. Martinez, 416 U.S. 396, 405–406 (1974).

19. See, in general, Ronald Berkman, *Opening the Gates: The Rise of the Prisoners' Movement* (1979).

20. 347 U.S. 483 (1954).

21. See, in general, Lawrence M. Friedman, *Your Time Will Come* (1985).

22. See 29 U.S.C. sec. 794: no "otherwise qualified handicapped individual" is to be excluded because of his handicap from any "program or activity receiving Federal financial assistance"; see also 20 U.S.C. sec. 1412 (education of handicapped children).

23. A student may, however, choose to have his case "heard entirely by the Dean of Students."

24. "Regulations Governing Student Conduct and Procedures for their Enforcement," Office of the President, Stanford University (1983).

25. Arthur H. Miller, "Political Issues and Trust in Government, 1964–1970," *American Political Sci. Rev.* 68 (1974):951.

26. *New York Times* (July 15, 1983), p. 1, col. 7.

27. Mark A. Peterson and George L. Priest, *The Civil Jury* (1982), p. 16; in San Francisco, the number of malpractice trials remained stable over the same period, but the percentage was greater than in Cook County: 7 percent of all civil trials. Michael G. Shanley and Mark A. Peterson, *Comparative Justice: Civil Jury Verdicts in San Francisco and Cook Counties, 1959–1980* (1983), p. 21.

28. 1975 Cal. Stat., 2nd Extraord. Sess., p. 3947.

29. Cal. Bus. & Prof. Code, sec. 6146; the section allows contingent fees of 40 percent of the first $50,000 recovered, 33⅓ percent of the next $50,000, 25 percent of the next $100,000, and

10 percent of amounts over $200,000. The section applies to all personal injury cases against "health care providers based upon . . . alleged professional negligence." See also Cal. Civ. Code sec. 3333.2 (no recovery for pain, suffering, disfigurement, and "other nonpecuniary damage" above $250,000).

30. David Mechanic, "Some Social Aspects of the Medical Malpractice Dilemma," *Duke Law Journal* (1975):1179, 1183.

31. There is a large literature on this late-nineteenth-century estrangement, loss of community, decline of rural values, and so on. See, in particular, Robert H. Wiebe, *The Search for Order, 1877–1920* (1967), especially ch. 3; and David M. Potter, "Social Cohesion and the Crisis of Law," *History and American Society: Essays of David M. Potter* (1973), p. 390.

32. The discussion of due process in this chapter, necessarily brief, leaves out the question whether people value due process for itself, or only as a means to some (substantive) end. No doubt it is usually the latter. People insist on procedures either as a kind of surrogate for substantive goals, or as a fall-back position—half a loaf, in other words. Environmentalists bedevil power companies and government agencies with procedural complaints, not because they have some attachment to regularity of process, but because delay and harassment may be their best chance to kill off an offensive power plant. People opposed to the death penalty, unsuccessful (of late) in getting anywhere with their program of total abolition, try to fight off each execution with endless procedural moves. In this regard, they have been much more successful. I am indebted here to comments made on an earlier draft by Robert Kagan.

PART II

6

AMERICAN LEGAL CHARACTER

T HE FIRST PART of this book discussed changes taking place in American legal culture, and connected those changes with developments in the legal system and in the texture of the law. "Legal culture" refers to public attitudes, norms, values, and ideas about the legal system; the theme of part I was the rise of new attitudes and norms—for example, the general expectation of justice. Part II asks whether these changes in legal culture affect the very "legal character" of Americans, and, in particular, ideas and practices relating to equality and inequality, style of life, and sexual behavior.

The subject is tricky. Not everybody shares the new attitudes; they are merely changes in central tendency. Often, slight changes in attitudes and values, and in small groups of people—that is, changes at the margin—can bring about what seem like big changes in society. It does not take many psychopaths to make the streets unsafe; five rapists can terrorize a medium-sized community; a handful of fanatic assassins can throw the whole state into an uproar. A society can be "claims-conscious" or litigious (compared to other societies) even if only a small percentage of the population presses claims or goes to court, just as a few thousand burglars (out of millions of people) generate a major "crime wave." A tremendous increase in claims-consciousness might (for example) only mean that the percentage of claims-conscious people in society has gone up from 1 to 2.

This point is worth stressing, because the discussion so far has been so speculative. There are some (weak) figures on litigation rates, but no quantitative data can support the argument on changes in attitudes toward law, and in the expectation of justice. Changes in formal law, and in the results of key cases, are clear enough; from these it is possible to infer changes in legal culture, though nothing in the process can be dignified with the name of "proof." Nor is there any way to know how general these changes in legal culture are. It would take only a few determined people to create the impression (and reality) of a claims-conscious society.

Legal culture and its norms also have been discussed in a very general way, and in isolation from political culture, economic status, and the general social context. But in real life, there is no such isolation; legal culture is part of general culture. Moreover, in society, ideas and opinions come in clusters: if we know that a person is bitterly opposed to legalized abortion, and is against gun control, we can predict, with reasonable accuracy, her opinions on a fair number of other subjects. She is likely to be a "conservative," and this means in turn that she is a person who holds a certain set of opinions. The same is true of a "liberal," a "radical," and so on. One can cut things down even finer: there are, to give a few examples, social liberals, economic conservatives, political liberals, and educational conservatives. There are clusters we expect to find more commonly in white liberals than in black ones; in Catholic conservatives but not in Protestant ones. And so it goes.

All this is obvious enough; and the same is true of opinions and attitudes about *law*, or what is called here American legal culture. There is not one culture, but many. There are legal conservatives, legal liberals, and all sorts of variants and subgroups. Within specific groups, legal culture consists of particular attitudes which, however, do tend to cohere, to hang together, to form clusters of related attitudes.

Study of these clusters has barely begun.[1] Historical study is, naturally, almost a total void, as far as survey data are concerned, although of course there are other kinds of evidence. In principle, one could write a separate history of the legal culture of every conceivable subgroup—men, women, whites, blacks, children, the elderly, Mormons, Irish-Americans, and so on. One also could question whether, because of the great diversity of peoples and types in this country, one can speak of an American legal character—a cluster of legal-cultural traits, different from the clusters that prevail in other societies.

To put it another way: there are many scholars who feel it makes sense to talk about "American character," elusive and subtle as this sort of thing may be;[2] similarly, it might be possible to talk about a segment of that character that specifically relates to legal behavior. This then would be (American) legal character. The term does not imply some kind of mystical *Volksgeist* or consensus. People have different opinions and norms about law, just as they do about everything else. All that is meant is that the bell-shaped curve of American ideas about law looks a little different, or has somewhat different values, than the bell-shaped curve for France, or Thailand, or America in 1855, for that matter. To say that women live longer than men, or that men are taller than women, is not to deny that there are tiny men who live to be 100; we are talking about the way men and women cluster on the bell-shaped curve. Moreover, height changes very little in adults, but opinions do change, and one person's views can infect somebody else's, especially in a community bounded by a single language or tradition.

Some people might doubt whether it is useful to use a concept like "legal character," just as some people are skeptical about the general idea of American character. But people certainly *talk* about legal character. What else does it mean to say that a society is "litigious," or that Americans are claims-conscious? There is an implicit comparison here, with other countries and with other times. The comparison relates to some sort of modal legal character, or, at the very least, to an increase in numbers of those who *do* possess some special or specific trait. Discussion of the due process revolution presupposed (among other things) new traits of legal culture—the general expectation of justice, for example. Another trait of legal culture was taken for granted: that the people who have expectations are willing to take concrete steps to see that their expectations are not disappointed, that justice is done.

This is claims-consciousness, or rights-consciousness. People assume that this trait has grown and become stronger over time. Actually, it is hard to pinpoint the exact form the trait takes and how general it is. Claims-consciousness in the United States does not seem to be directed only at courts, and it is less the result of some sort of character trait (or deficiency), some national feistiness, than it is the result of certain social changes. One of these changes is the reduction of general uncertainty, which has reverberated throughout the legal culture. This does not rule out the notion that there is something odd or extraordinary about American behavior. Americans certainly *seem* more law-minded (though not more law-abiding) than other people. Perhaps this is merely an illusion. There is so little decent cross-cultural research that it is hard to do more than speculate.[3]

The idea of claims-consciousness or rights-consciousness, at least in the popular press, lacks a certain clarity of focus. The core idea is one of modal character: it implies that there is a large, or typical, group of Americans who are not deferential to authority; who have a keen sense of what is coming to them and are willing to take action to get it. Of course, such people definitely exist. But in the first place, as mentioned earlier, it does not take many of them to create a "claims explosion"; in the second place, nobody has any idea whether legal character has changed over the years, in the sense of underlying personality traits. What *has* changed is opportunity structure and social context. Everything beyond that is guesswork.

Even modern survey evidence has to be taken with caution. O'Connell and Simon found that 70 percent of the people injured in accidents had "no knowledge or expectation of payment for pain and suffering."[4] This does not exclude the possibility that they then learned to expect it (from lawyers or relatives); or that the 30 percent who did know of or expected payment represent some kind of quantum leap over the percentage of similar victims a hundred years ago who had such expectations.

We are, of course, in the dark about these ancestors. The literature often describes the "hardy pioneers" in terms that fit the modern claim pusher. Perhaps the same type of person who once boldly crossed mountains and deserts in a covered wagon is today badgering the Veteran's Administration or dragging Sears, Roebuck into court. As noted in chapter 2, it is hard to find solid evidence of a rise in litigation rates over time. Some nineteenth-century writers described the Western fringes of settlement as incurably litigious. Joseph Baldwin, writing about the old Southwest in the early nineteenth century, claimed that in Sumpter County, Alabama, in one year, "some four or five thousand suits, in the common-law courts alone, were brought. . . . The white *suable* population of Sumpter was then some 2,400 men." There was an even heavier amount of suing in the "lower or river counties of Mississippi." It was, in short, a "merry time" for lawyers like young Baldwin. "We brightened up mightily, and shook our quills joyously, like goslings in the midst of a shower. . . . Law and lawing soon got to be the staple productions of the country."[5]

In the early colonial period, too, participation in activities of local courts was almost universal. The names of most adult males could be found somewhere on the court records, as litigants or witnesses, in almost any given year, as a study of Accomack County, Virginia, showed.[6] Yet nobody takes this as a symptom of claims-consciousness. It is rather an index of the meaning of these courts in that particular society. It is not surprising to find that people take their problems to court when court is cheap and accessible. The cost of justice is a variable that must be (and usually is not) taken into account. Besides, these colonial "courts" were more than courts in the modern sense; they were all-purpose agencies of government. Much of what appears in the pages of the court records was hardly "litigation"; in the old colonial courts, estates were probated, cattle brands recorded, written documents spread on the record, taxes levied, roads laid out or repairs ordered, and so on.

Individualism and Equality

It is right to be cautious, then, in putting forward the idea that claims-consciousness or rights-consciousness has increased over time or that it affects Americans in general. Whether or not the general impression that Americans are getting more and more claims-conscious is true is impossible to say. What is reasonably clear is the type of claim that helps give rise to the impression. The reduction of uncertainty and the rise of the welfare state raised expectations for justice and fair treatment, and blurred the distinction between what was and what was not appropriate for legal treatment. There is no need, then, to posit any change in underlying "character."

Still, it is useful to confront an apparent paradox. When we talk about people who "stick up for their rights," we generally have a particular personality type in mind—the rugged individualist, the nonconformist, somebody marching to his own drummer. But common opinion often runs in exactly the opposite direction: that we live in an age of "conformity," an age of "other-directed" people;[7] the rugged individualist lived in the good old days of the nineteenth century and is now virtually extinct.

None of this should be taken too literally. "Conformity" and "individualism" are slippery words. Everybody is an individual; everybody is also a conformist. There are no social surveys to speak of for the nineteenth century. What is known about peoples' ideas comes from other kinds of records—diaries, letters, magazine articles. These are not necessarily good guides to what the vast majority of people thought, that is, those who did not keep diaries or write letters or magazine articles.

Still, there is value in watching how literature and written records describe ideals or models among citizens in different periods. What nineteenth-century writers thought about the self-made man is an important clue to the underlying concept of the individual. Indeed, "self-made man" is an interesting phrase. Precisely what did the self-made man make himself into? Certainly not a hippie; not a free spirit; not a rebel; not an isolate. On the contrary, the self-made man (the self-made woman was unthinkable or undesirable) was the very model of bourgeois morality. The self-made man had the Protestant ethic. He was early to bed and early to rise. He worked hard, built up a business, drank moderately or not at all, had a conventional family life, did not engage in too much sex, went to church, supported charity. He could function in a free society without external controls precisely because controls over his behavior were so firmly internalized. He was an individualist who suppressed his idiosyncrasies. He might take risks in business, but in other regards he made his way within the framework of the established order.

Of course, just as "pioneers" were always a small minority, self-made men who went from rags to riches, from log cabin to mighty mansion, were also a tiny handful. But there is some evidence in social history that suggests the power of the ideal in the lives of the broader middle class. There is, for example, some evidence that the population as a whole became more "civilized" in the nineteenth century. At any rate, serious crime probably declined in the course of the century.[8] There was perhaps a change in sexual morality, too—fornication may have dropped off, at least on the evidence of one study. Fornication is not easy to measure; but Smith and Hindus tried to get at the frequency of this behavior by counting numbers of children born too soon after their parents' wedding to be full-term babies.[9] This and other scraps of evidence tend to suggest that middle-class morality, conventional morality, spread downward (and upward?) in society in the course of the century.

Another interesting bit of evidence is provided by John Philip Reid's study of legal behavior on the grim overland trail to California and Oregon in the middle of the century.[10] Reid argues that this part of the frontier was far from lawless. The men and women who struggled across the American wilderness showed an amazing respect for law, for property, and for order. The norms they followed were customs, or, if you will, norms of living law; there was no organized government, no police, no obvious enforcement mechanism in wild mountain and desert country. On the other side of the coin, the nineteenth century had strikingly little respect for people who were "individuals" in a different sense from Horatio Alger. The unattached, marginal person was the object of fear and disgust. Society loathed and mistreated transients and paupers; the "tramp" stood lowest of all in the social scale.[11]

In some ways, the modern individualist is the exact opposite of the nineteenth-century individual. At the very least, the free spirit, the social deviant, suffers less social and legal ostracism today than his nineteenth-century counterpart. The "individual" now might be someone who does not "conform"; someone who builds his own life, her own personality; who makes the most of his own uniqueness. Literature and the popular press put less stress on self-discipline and self-control. Outside the Bible Belt, adult chastity or sexual abstinence is hardly the ideal it used to be. Today the emphasis is on "maximizing one's potential." There are plenty of workaholics around, and even some ascetics, but there is more toleration for "doing your own thing," for variations in life-style.

Of course, the press (and gossip) tend to exaggerate the deviant, colorful, titillating aspects of modern behavior. The "new morality" makes good copy for television and magazines. Most people's lives are probably still governed by humdrum inner rules. Still, social indicators do suggest a real shift in behavior, and thus we cannot rule out changes in modal personality. The rise in cohabitation, as recorded in census data, is one such indicator. Another indicator, as I will argue, is change in American law.

On the assumption that the changes in behavior and in ideology are real, the question of why such changes have taken place naturally arises. This is a difficult question, and there is no way to answer it comprehensively. But surely reduction in the level of uncertainty (discussed in part I) is an important factor. It is certainly plausible to think that at least some Americans who lived in the shadow of uncertainty would respond to those conditions of life in particular patterned ways, and that these patterns would change as uncertainties diminished. Facts of life in 1800 or 1850 might push people in the direction of timidity and conformity. There would be fear of excessive individuality, fear of striking out on one's own, especially for the poor, and all those below top levels of society.

The myth of the frontiersman, the hardy pioneer, the rugged individualist, points in the opposite direction. But how common were such people? By and large, a dependent person is . . . dependent. He or she is likely to bow to authority. Probably *most* American slaves behaved like slaves; most women respected and obeyed men; most children followed the wishes and whims of their parents; most workers were docile and helpless. Of course, people were socialized into their roles; habits of obedience were drummed into their heads from an early age. But, in addition, the price of rebellion was high; most people must have felt they could not afford to pay it.

The modern cocoon of security makes a kind of freedom more possible, and opens the door to personal adventure for more people than before. After all, it requires less courage for Americans to hitchhike through India in an age of penicillin, vaccination, and travelers' checks than it took for Englishmen to tramp through the African bush in the nineteenth century, when many of these explorers would never come back. It took more guts to follow the overland trail to California in the 1850s than it takes today to buzz out in an air-conditioned car from Kansas City to San Francisco on the Interstate. People who, thanks to what might be called the social "safety net," need not immediately fear missing a meal when out of work may be more willing to quit a job and try something new than somebody with a well-grounded fear of the poor-house or starvation.

All this, of course, is conjecture. In the nineteenth century, millions of people crossed the Atlantic to begin a new life in America even though the trip was hard and dangerous and meant cutting themselves off from home and family. Thousands of immigrants took the overland trail to Oregon and California in the face of great suffering and at the risk of death. Of course, there were also risks in staying put, and sheer desperation drove many migrants on their course, just as millions of refugees then and now undertake impossible journeys because of war, grinding poverty, or murderous oppression. There was no lack of quiet courage in nineteenth-century society. Whether there was more or less than today, or the same amount, is unknown. But certain behaviors took more courage then—in particular, striking out for a bold, new, "individual" life. This once meant risk of suffering and death. Some risks and adventures are not what they used to be.

Life in the United States and other Western countries today presupposes modern medicine, the welfare state, and the social "safety net." This is a social environment that encourages (or at least does not stifle) individualism of the modern sort, the individualism of "doing your own thing." This is perhaps a more radical breed of individualism than the nineteenth century tolerated. The cliche is often heard that people today want security, as if this were wicked of them. Security, however, does not necessarily mean a cozy nook; it can also mean a kind of base camp from which the climber can storm a very high and dangerous mountain. Security can include a kind of freedom to experiment. In this regard, the phrase "safety net" is particularly apt. A safety net encourages some people to swing on the trapeze, or walk the tight-rope, who would otherwise not dare.

Thus the new individualism is related, too, to the interdependence of modern society. The various "safety nets," which encourage individualism, are public programs that proceed from a cycle of demands and responses, which in turn presuppose that state of interdependence. To depend on somebody is to expect more from them. Master and slave have their own breed of mutuality; but there is also the inter-

dependency of equals, a network of reciprocal expectations. Relationships of reciprocity exist in every society. Reciprocity is what makes a
society tick; the precise form is what differentiates one society from
another. In modern society people depend—must depend—on the
behavior of strangers; they expect a reciprocity that they cannot enforce
on their own. From this comes a kind of collective decision that the
generalized third party (the state, the law) must intervene. Only law
can efficiently enforce the other side of many important bargains.

When a person buys a car "from" General Motors, he does not deal
directly with the company. He buys it through a dealer, who is far
removed in space and authority from the factory or the company's
headquarters. The buyer exchanges money for a commodity (the car),
which he hopes will be safe and well made. But he has no way to
enforce those expectations on a face-to-face basis. For that, he needs
law, or thinks he does. And, of course, in time he comes to expect
third-party rules, and third-party enforcement. Expectations go up,
even though the buyer is in a sense more dependent on the car company than on the man who might have sold him a horse in the
nineteenth century. The "dependence" is not because there is no
alternative to General Motors (there is); but because the safety and
economy of the car are beyond the buyer's power, no matter who sells
it. It is in this sense that the buyer is dependent, and his expectations
go up precisely for this reason; indeed, these are two sides of the very
same coin.

Thus there is a link between "individualism" and the cycle of expectations that lies behind the demand for total justice. The expectations
create demands that lead to the programs that foster "individualism."
This "individualism" is also linked to the supposed claims-
consciousness of Americans. Here too the "safety net" (in the broadest
sense) has an impact. People have more to gain from pressing their
claims than was true in the past—but there is also less to lose. Anyone
who dared sue the boss in the nineteenth century lost his job. A
teacher who complained about work conditions never got another
contract. The private who talked back to the sergeant was court-
martialed. A defendant who started talking about "due process" in the
police station felt the back of the nightstick. All this of course has
changed. Nobody thinks it odd any more that a worker can strike or sue
and stay on the payroll; that tenants in a giant housing complex can

attack the landlord's policies and stay put in their flats; that a professor can sue her university for sex discrimination and continue to draw a paycheck.

It is worth repeating that this argument relates primarily to the United States and, presumably, to other Western, urbanized, industrial countries. Only these countries seem to have produced, or allowed, the cycle of demands, responses, and expectations that characterize "modern" legal culture. The situation in the People's Republic of China or the Soviet Union is probably dramatically different. Socialist and authoritarian societies do not permit the cycle to go forward; they try to hold expectations and demands in check, tightly capped and controlled. The stimuli to change are often the same as in the West, but the social responses are different. To deal adequately with legal culture in these societies would be a separate, very difficult task, which this book will leave to other hands.

Equality

Modern individualism has, of course, all sorts of reflections in law, as well as in culture generally. It has, for example, an obvious impact on how law treats sexual morality, the subject of the following chapter. It has also affected the working meaning of a key concept in American legal culture (and in society), the concept of equality. Equality no longer means primarily equality before the law; it has acquired a broader, deeper meaning. The new meaning runs roughly as follows: Every person has the right not to suffer any handicap or disadvantage, in life or law, because of "immutable" characteristics (race, sex, physical disability, old age), or because of way of life (even choice of sexual partners), or because of those mixtures of choice and birth called ethnicity and religion. I will call this revised social definition *plural equality*.

The subject here is popular ideas—ideas held by masses of people, whether they think about these ideas a lot or a little, or whether they think about them at all. The working assumption is that ideas of this kind—the raw material of popular culture, and thus of both political and legal culture can influence or shape concrete behavior, which in turn creates the structure and substance of living law.

There are also, of course, at any given time, more formal, high-level writings and philosophies in circulation. The higher culture can influence popular ideas. It is also reasonable to assume that the higher culture reflects popular ideas—it uses the ordinary culture uncon-sciously, as clay and bricks from which to build its systems. In the hands of thinkers, popular ideas are transformed; they become more rational, more systematic, more profound, just as a great composer can make a symphony out of motives drawn from folk music.

But the formative element in law is not the high legal culture; it is the general legal culture. By "general legal culture" I do not necessar-ily mean the culture of the man and woman in the street, of the "majority," or of "typical" people. I mean attitudes and values held by people who exert explicit or implicit pressure on the legal system, who press explicit or implicit demands. These might be, and often are, rich and powerful people, rather than "the masses," but they are not profes-sional deep thinkers. I emphasize this point, and also the postulate that ordinary legal culture does not mean the legal culture of "simple" people; it is rather the legal ideas and attitudes of those outside higher culture, which includes manufacturers, doctors, even United States senators. This legal culture need not be deep, or rational, or system-atic, or internally consistent. Usually it is none of these things.

A theory of plural equality underlies modern legal culture. This "theory" is not necessarily a good theory. It would have a lot of trouble holding its own against sustained, rational critique. But it is still of vast importance. Popular theories are almost always muddled and unclear. Take, for example, the concept of "immutable" characteristics. Sex and race are outstanding instances. The Supreme Court itself puts stress on "immutability" in the logic of constitutional decision. Thus, in *Frontiero* v. *Richardson*, one of the key decisions on sex discrimina-tion, the Court remarked that "sex, like race and national origin, is an immutable characteristic determined solely by the accident of birth."[12] It was therefore especially odious to impose "special disabilities" on people because of this "immutable" aspect, their sex.

But what does it mean to say that a trait is "immutable?" There are three meanings. Something can be immutable because it is a fact that nobody can undo. It would be offensive if the law discriminated against people born in Chicago; once born there, there is nothing one can do to be born some other place. This is, perhaps, the sense in which national origin is "immutable."

"Immutable" can also be used in two other senses, one biological and one social. Some characteristics are fixed and unchangeable because they are part of a biological program. The interaction between body and event—in an accident for example—can bring about an irreversible physical handicap. A biological meaning is the dominant one in people's minds; it is what the Supreme Court, for example, means when it talks about immutability. But in fact most legally relevant "immutable" characteristics are immutable mainly in the third, social sense; they are immutable only because social definitions are slow to change, and because the individual cannot alter them. Personal efforts do not make a dent on them; they change only in the course of social transformation.

The leopard, to be sure, cannot change his spots, and people cannot control race and sex. But this does not mean that race and sex are really matters of biology, in the senses that underlie social conflict and controversy. Race is almost entirely a matter of social definition. To begin with, biologically speaking, millions of American "blacks" are not black at all. They are white people with a black ancestor here and there. Why a person who is three-quarters white and one-quarter black is "black" instead of "white" is not a question a biologist can answer; nothing about this racial classification is genetic. It is, however, part of the legal definition of race, and was spelled out explicitly, for example, in southern statutes in the days of slavery.[13]

Whatever the biological basis, race as defined is an important trait socially; the social definition of race, not the biological definition, is the crucial feature. The racial label attached to an American plainly has critical consequences. Of course, there *are* biological differences between, for example, people who are largely of Caucasian ancestry, and those who are black or Oriental. But the question is, why are these differences relevant? Hair color is a physical, genetic trait that differs from person to person, group to group. But it is not treated as a significant basis for assigning human beings to classes; skin color and its related traits are. The reasons have nothing to do with biology. This is clear when one notes how important language is in assigning human beings to groups. What language you speak is almost entirely the product of social factors (some of them "immutable" in the first sense discussed).

Sex differences of course have a deeper biological basis than race differences. People are born male or female, and ever since the dawn of the species (even earlier to be sure), anatomy has been destiny for women and men. But even here the most blatant aspects of sex roles, the most controverted questions of behavior and status, are matters of social definition. No man can breastfeed a baby, but nothing genetic keeps him from changing a diaper, or bars a woman from mining coal or running the state.

Ideas of who is, and ought to be, equal to whom, and in what regard, are socially defined and are subject to constant change. Why, then, is it important that people not suffer because of "immutable" characteristics? It is because people feel that no one should be disadvantaged by virtue of actions, behaviors, or traits that are not that person's "fault." This is a corollary of the axiom of total justice. "Immutability" gets cast in biological terms, because people (including judges) find it easier to think in such terms; the social definition of most "immutable" traits is a more subtle and sophisticated matter. But a social definition is just as much beyond the individual's power to change as a biological definition. And there is a certain danger in biologizing traits. It helps keep alive the idea of important inborn differences between races and sexes beyond those real differences written into the body by genetic laws.

A century ago, Americans also professed a strong belief in equality and in equal rights before the law. But social norms—and the law— defined equality quite differently from the current definition. Inborn and "immutable" characters were part of a person's fate; they were part of a package that birth, luck, and destiny delivered. Nobody expected total justice; ethnicity, religion, race, and sex were part of a natural pattern of caprice (and injustice, if you will). Today sex, race, ethnicity, and so on, are still beyond felt power to change, but many people feel strongly that no one should suffer disadvantage on account of these traits. Thus, the doctrine that what is "immutable" should be legally irrelevant has been raised to a constitutional principle, and recast and redefined in ways that make blazingly apparent the injustice of the older view.

Equality and Its Transformations

In 1800, or 1850, or 1900, the United States was a "free" country, with a Bill of Rights, and mass political participation; people were proud of our democratic institutions. Yet in many obvious ways, legal equality was severely limited. In 1850, for example, only white adult males could vote or hold office. Women had limited rights and a very subordinate role in society. A married woman was especially handicapped at law. She was basically under her husband's economic control. He held the title to her property and had full power to manage and deal with the marital estate. A married woman could not buy or sell property without her husband's participation; she could not even make a will. The so-called Married Women's Property Laws gradually lifted these disabilities. But few of these laws were passed before 1850, and they brought about only small changes in the economic power of married women.[14] No woman practiced law before the 1870s, and women did not vote in national elections until about the time of the first World War.

The black population was in an even worse position. Most southern blacks were slaves; northern blacks, and free blacks in the South, were voteless, despised, and oppressed. The dominant population felt, quite generally, that these arrangements were part of the order of nature; blacks were inferior beings, unfit for civilized society. Equality, then, mostly meant formal rights, and mostly among adult white males. Others in society had rights of a distinctly lesser kind. For example, a woman had the right to a fair trial in serious criminal cases. Even slaves had certain rights, in theory at least, in criminal cases.

There were important distinctions among white males as well. Some were more equal than others. There clearly was a dominant group—roughly, Protestants from northern European backgrounds. Their dominance was not formally recognized; it was not written into law (with some exceptions); indeed, the law on the whole tried to look scrupulously neutral. But living law inevitably reflected the climate of opinion in the country at large, and here it was clear who was on top, and who was not.

People generally are quite unaware of the full range of their assumptions and prejudices. In the nineteenth century, the dominant class was pleased with itself, and proud of America's achievement. De Tocqueville, among others, was amazed at the patriotic zeal of Americans. People believed they lived in the land of the free, a country with liberty and justice for all. Yet, rights "belonged" most deeply, by tradition and merit, to a core group, the "real" Americans. Equal rights meant freedom and toleration for other people who might come to live here (with slaves a conspicuous exception). Outsiders and newcomers had legal equality, formal equality; they did not have social or moral equality.

Essentially, then, this was a country that belonged to white, Christian men from northern Europe. The acknowledged norms of the country were their norms; their code of ethics was the code that had official recognition. In the 1850s, Joseph H. Lumpkin, justice of the Georgia Supreme Court, in a famous case on the rights of free blacks, put the matter this way: "Our ancestors settled this State . . . as a community of white men, professing the christian religion, and possessing an equality of rights and privileges."[15] Blacks were "a race of Pagan slaves"; they could never rise, whether as slaves or free blacks, to "parity of rank" with whites. Note that the phrases Lumpkin used— "community of white men . . . christian religion"—excluded others as well as blacks, perhaps unconsciously.

Leading citizens probably agreed on the whole with Lumpkin— even northern abolitionists. They took the goals, standards, and norms of white Christian men, especially Protestants from northern Europe, as the goals, standards, and norms of the United States. Polygamy, for example, was a crime, even though in large parts of the world it was normal, accepted practice. Cultural relativity was not a strong point in the nineteenth century, as the Mormons discovered the hard way. Every legal system makes choices among conflicting norms; the nineteenth-century choice was narrow and largely unconscious.

No doubt lawyers in the nineteenth and early twentieth centuries sincerely shared in the national sense of pride. Here was a legal system in which a poor Chinese laundryman could defeat the bigots of San Francisco in the highest court of the land. This case, *Yick Wo* v. *Hopkins* (1886), was indeed one of the Supreme Court's shining hours.[16] Other decisions were by no means so laudable, by our lights. And the same lawyers who patted themselves on the back over *Yick Wo* may have seen nothing wrong with Chinese exclusion—that is, with laws that kept Chinese out of the country and prevented them from becoming citizens. After all, as a speaker in the California Constitutional Convention of 1878–1879 put it, the Chinese were a debased and debasing people. They were "unfit for assimilation with people of our race."[17]

No worse charge could be leveled at an ethnic group, in that period, than this: they could not "assimilate." "Assimilate" meant to conform to values and standards of the dominant group. The Chinese, in short, did not belong in this country. Chinese who were born here, and were citizens by birth, necessarily enjoyed the basic rights of Americans. But Chinese exclusion underscored that these were second-hand rights. They belonged above all to somebody else.

Today this attitude seems inconsistent, even hypocritical; but that is because we now see the world through the lens of plural equality. The nineteenth-century mind worked otherwise. For example, it was commonly said that the United States was a "Christian country." What could this mean? First of all, it is clear what it did *not* mean. It did not mean that Christianity, or any part of it, was the established or official church, though that had been the case in some of the colonies. It also did not mean, most emphatically, that people who professed other religions—Jews, Moslems, Buddhists—and nonbelievers, did not have full civil and religious rights. The irreligious had the right, constitutionally protected, to ignore religion; and religious minorities had the right to build temples, mosques, synagogues, and churches and worship exactly as they pleased.

The nineteenth century did not recognize a state religion, but there was, in fact, a prevailing religion: Christianity, and in particular its Protestant branches. America began and continued as a "community of Christians"; Christians made this a free country, and granted to others their basic rights. It was Christianity, too, which was considered, as Joseph Story put it, "a part of the common law."[18]

One sign of this attitude in the law itself was the concept of blasphemy, an interesting (now vanished) crime. Essentially, blasphemy meant ridiculing or defaming Christianity. It was a capital offense in colonial Massachusetts. Under a Maryland law of 1723 (ch. 16), any person who "wittingly," in speech or writing, did "blaspheme or curse God, or deny our Saviour Jesus Christ to be the Son of God, or shall deny the Holy Trinity, the Father, Son and Holy Ghost," was liable, for the first offense, to be "bored through the tongue"; for the second offense, to be "stigmatized by burning in the forehead with the letter B"; for the third offense, to be put to death.

Blasphemy statutes did not disappear after the Revolution. They survived the disestablishment of churches, and remained on the books in many states throughout the nineteenth century. Few people, apparently, saw any conflict between these laws and the Bill of Rights, or freedom of religion. In these states blasphemy was always defined in Christian terms; no law guarded the dignity of Buddha or Mohammed. Christianity thus had a special legal status. This was sometimes made explicit in other ways as well. Until 1877, under Article Six of the Bill of Rights of New Hampshire, the legislature could authorize towns and cities to "make adequate provision . . . for the support and maintenance of public Protestant teachers of piety, religion, and morality." A constitutional convention in 1876 got rid of this clause, but at least one delegate stoutly defended it: "That word 'Protestant' makes no war upon any denomination whatever . . . Gentile, Greek, Mormon, or any one else. It is simply there to express the regard of the people of New Hampshire for religious institutions."[19]

The blasphemy cases, too, are quite revealing. In *State* v. *Chandler* (1837),[20] a Delaware case, a man named Thomas Jefferson Chandler, "seduced by the instigation of the devil," stated "in the presence and hearing of divers citizens," that "the virgin Mary was a whore and Jesus Christ was a bastard." He was convicted of blasphemy; on appeal the conviction was affirmed. The blasphemy law was valid, because it tended toward preservation of order, in an overwhelmingly Christian country. Defendant was punished (said the court), "not for his offence against his God, but for his offence against man, whose peace and safety . . . was endangered by such conduct." A "sound" distinction could be drawn between "a religion preferred by law, and a religion preferred by the people, without coercion of law." When people profess a "creed freely chosen" by themselves, they may "claim the protection of law" for its "full and perfect enjoyment." If the people of Delaware chose Islam or the religion of "Joe Smith," the law would protect those religions against civil unrest, through blasphemy laws.[21] Christianity had a special place in law, in other words, because of its special position in society.

In another well-known case, *People* v. *Ruggles* (New York, 1811),[22]

Chancellor Kent put the matter in a sightly different light: "Nor are we bound . . . as some have strangely supposed, either not to punish at all, or to punish indiscriminately the like attacks upon the religion of *Mahomet* or of the grand *Lama*; and for this plain reasons, that . . . we are a christian people, and the morality of the country is deeply ingrafted upon christianity, and not upon the doctrines or worship of those imposters." No judge today, it hardly needs to be said, would refer to Mohammed, or even the Dalai Lama, as an "imposter," whatever the judge's secret thoughts.[23]

The language issue can serve as another illustration of the meaning of equality in the American past. Nothing in the Constitution makes English the official language of the country. In fact, the Supreme Court held, in a famous case in 1923, that Nebraska had no power to prohibit schools from teaching foreign languages to children (German, in that case).[24] But *the* language of the country has always been English, and this is clearly understood. National policy toward such linguistic minorities as native Americans or Puerto Ricans has hardly been a model of enlightenment. Theodore Roosevelt probably expressed the view of most people in 1919, when he said that "We have room for but one language here and that is the English language, for we intend to see that the crucible turns our people out as Americans and not as dwellers in a polyglot boarding house."[25]

In the past century or so, the older conception of equality has moved quite dramatically in the direction of plural equality. The civil rights movement has led the way. There have been radical adjustments in race relations. In the long run the attack on sex discrimination and the redefinition of sex roles may be even more important. These two developments are so significant in their own right that they tend to obscure the more general change, the shift toward plural equality.

Blasphemy laws are only a dot on the map of history, but their fate is instructive. As late as 1921, a court in Maine upheld a conviction for blasphemy. The "religion of Christ," said the court, was the "prevailing religion of this country"; it was therefore proper to punish someone who treated "the God of the Christian religion, or the Holy Scriptures with contempt and ridicule."[26] By 1970, such notions were, legally speaking, as quaint as high-buttoned shoes. In *State* v. *West*,[27] a Maryland court declared the state blasphemy statute unconstitutional. Maryland, said the court, could not constitutionally "extend its protec-

tive cloak to the Christian religion or to any other religion." In a very
few states, blasphemy statutes sit rotting away among the statutes, but
blasphemy is not part of America's living law.

Meanwhile, the Supreme Court, in a sweeping series of cases,
strengthened the "wall of separation" between church and state. The
wall became quite high and thick.[28] Details do not concern us, nor the
exact limits of the court's doctrines. What is important is the underlying ethos. The United States seems to be, on the whole, a religious
country, at least as compared to other Western nations. There is a
good deal more churchgoing here than in most of Europe. But there is
no longer the same recognition of a "prevailing" religion. The Supreme Court does not tolerate overtly Christian prayer in public
schools; indeed, it does not tolerate any sort of prayer, even the most
denatured and "nondenominational" sort.[29]

The school prayer decisions of the 1960s, according to public opinion polls, are quite unpopular. But they have lasted a full generation;
even a popular president (Ronald Reagan) has been unable to convince
Congress to override the Court. And even those who speak out for
prayer in public schools admit that these cannot be openly Christian
prayers. School prayer would have to take minority religions into account, and the schools would also have to respect the rights of the
nonreligious. Most Americans are still Christians, often fervent ones;
most Americans are also white. There cannot be a "prevailing" religion, any more than there can be a "prevailing" race or sex.

The historical shift is underscored when one looks at the difference
in tone between two important cases, decided by the Supreme Court a
century apart, but worlds apart in legal culture. *Reynolds* v. *United
States* (1878), arose under a federal law which made polygamy a crime
in the territories.[30] The law was directed specifically against the Mormons concentrated in Utah and surrounding territories. The Mormons practiced polygamy as part of their religion. Reynolds, the defendant, was a Mormon in Utah Territory. He was convicted of polygamy
and appealed, pleading freedom of religion.

The Supreme Court affirmed his conviction. Reynold's religious
beliefs, said the court, were no excuse for polygamy. The constitution
protected freedom of religion, but not everything could be justified in
the name of religion: "suppose one believed that human sacrifices were
a necessary part of religious worship"; or suppose "a wife religiously

believed it was her duty to burn herself upon the funeral pile of her dead husband." No one would "seriously contend" that these dreadful acts were protected, in the name of religious freedom.[31]

The court assumed, of course, that polygamy was as obnoxious as human sacrifice. Yet Mormon polygamy took nobody's life and was more or less a victimless crime. In a revealing passage, the Court explained its views further: polygamy had "always been odious among the northern and western nations of Europe, and, until the establishment of the Mormon Church, was almost exclusively a feature of the life of Asiatic and of African people."[32] The court took it for granted that standards of "Asiatic and . . . African people" had less claim on law than standards of "northern and western nations of Europe." Probably few people disagreed.

Wisconsin v. *Yoder* (1972)[33] stands in sharp contrast to *Reynolds*. Here the court dealt again with a minority religion. The defendants, Jonas Yoder, Wallace Miller, and Adin Yutzy, were Amish people, living in Wisconsin. The Amish refused to send their children to high school; in their view, eight grades were enough. They based their antipathy to high school on religious grounds. Children, according to the Amish, did not need high school education. The Amish wanted their children trained to be "productive members of the Amish community"; they saw no reason to train them to be members of the outside world. If Amish children went to high school, they risked their very "salvation."

The Amish were thus making a claim of a rather extreme type. They were not asking for the right to run their own high schools. They wanted no high school at all. They denied the state's right to require any education past eighth grade. Yet the Supreme Court ruled in their favor. The opinion (written by Chief Justice Burger) praised the Amish way of life. The Amish had "an excellent record as law-abiding and generally self-sufficient members of society." The community was "a highly successful social unit within our society, even if apart from the conventional 'mainstream.' "[34] (This of course was also true of the Mormons.) The Court refused to force high-school education on the Amish.

There are, to be sure, all sorts of differences—technical, legal, and social—between *Reynolds* and *Yoder*. But the main difference is one of legal culture. What had changed was an attitude toward the prevailing culture: the right to enforce a single, dominant social code. In the course of the century, the justices of the Supreme Court, like millions of other citizens, had learned to tolerate other ways of life, ways once considered primitive, barbaric, strange. But the *Yoder* decision goes beyond mere "toleration." Public education (or *any* high-school education) would threaten the Amish community. Compulsory schooling, according to some of the testimony, could "result in great psychological harm to Amish children." It might produce "conflicts," and ultimately even bring about "the destruction of the Old Order Amish church community." Education could "undermine" traditional religion, and force the Amish to "be assimilated into society at large."[35] In the nineteenth century, "assimilation into society at large" (meaning the dominant community) was taken to be a positive good, a valid goal of public policy. Not so (or not to the same degree) in the 1970s.

A recent study by two political scientists explored high court cases on the meaning of the "free exercise" clause, which is part of the First Amendment. In some of these cases marginal religions (sects) were involved; in some, mainstream religions. Surprisingly, sects did better in these court cases than mainstream religions. There are problems with the data, to be sure; the cases turn on different facts and are hard to compare. But marginal religions are certainly bolder than in the past in demanding recognition, and courts seen inclined to give them what they wish.[36] This tendency goes back, perhaps, to the famous flag-salute cases of the 1940s. Children of members of Jehovah's Witnesses refused to salute the flag in school, on religious grounds. The Supreme Court, in the first of these cases, sustained a school rule that forced the children to salute. Three years later, the Court reversed itself. The case turned more on freedom of speech than on freedom of religion, but the attitude of the court was significant. If there is any "fixed star" in the constitutional "constellation," said Justice Jackson, writing for the majority, it is that "no official . . . can prescribe what shall be orthodox in politics . . . religion, or other matters of opinion."[37]

Of course, the Supreme Court, all other courts, and every agency of law necessarily enforce *some* moral code. It is impossible to imagine a legal system which is truly "neutral" toward religious beliefs, ethical codes, and ways of life. The legal system did and does enforce prevailing moral standards; it cannot help it. Moreover, the *Reynolds* case still represents the law in important regards. A religion that called for human sacrifice, or suicide, or burning widows would get no help from the First Amendment. This would probably still be true of polygamy as well. Bob Jones University found that "freedom of religion" did not entitle it to a tax exemption so long as it practiced what some regarded as racial discrimination. [38]

Still, the differences between *Reynolds* and *Yoder* are striking. Courts (and citizens in general) are now more sensitive to pluralism, more aware of alternative outlooks, more willing to concede their legitimacy. There is a band, a range of codes that more or less coexist. The new attitude shows up in large and small ways. There is less insistence on dress codes at school and on the job. Most employers and government agencies would allow a worker to wear a turban at the office, if this were defined as a religious practice. Tolerance, of course, has limits; the employer probably would not allow a swimsuit or a gorilla suit, no matter what excuse the worker gave. It is never true that "anything goes."

The evidence of a legal culture has been drawn by and large from court opinions, which is hardly a random sample of attitudes. But internal legal culture is in many ways a mirror of external culture; at least part of the general community must share those attitudes that shape the case-law. Opinion polls suggest great changes in majority opinions about minority rights. [39] There has been a tremendous decline in overt, public racism. Prejudice remains, but even driving it underground is a major social achievement.

Even more important are changes in the way minorities think of themselves, how they define equality, how they seek to achieve it. The black population, for example, looks far beyond formal equality; blacks do not accept a subordinate role in a society which is not theirs and which merely "tolerates" them or grudgingly grants "rights." They have been seized by a passionate new vision of equality whose key feature is a radical denial of the premises of the old equality. They, and other minorities, do not concede the right of the majority to social or moral hegemony. The minorities insist that they are, or ought to be, on a par with the majority. And why not?

The very style, the terms of public discourse—the rules of the legal game—reflect plural equality. Modern judges or lawyers would wince at lines like those quoted from the *Reynolds* case about "Asiatic and African peoples." A court could well reach the same result; but the grounds and the language would have to be different. Judges and lawyers—like public officials generally, and probably much of the white population—know they have to show respect for "Asiatic and African peoples," just as they must respect the rights and views of women, old people, the retarded, prisoners, and so on. Legislators are willing to pass civil rights laws on a scale unheard of in the past: buildings are built to accommodate wheelchairs; ballots and drivers' tests are printed in Spanish; Native Americans are no longer called "primitive" or "savages." The country seems to regret, belatedly, the slaughter and dispossession of the tribes and the ruthless attempts to stamp out language and culture, to "assimilate" these groups into the melting pot. Underlying all of these changes is the more general one: the redefinition of equality in America.

To sum up: in nineteenth-century legal culture, equality did not mean pluralism. Leading citizens did not think of their county as a kind of confederation of groups, all of equal worth and with equally valid cultures. Nineteenth-century equality meant rights for guests who lived in somebody else's house. Twentieth-century pluralism has moved boldly toward a broader concept. Equality now *does mean* a confederation of groups. And each group has an ownership stake in the house; all more or less are tenants in common.

It is easy to see that the new concept has tremendous implications for law. The old rights were narrow, circumscribed, limited; minorities were expected to keep their place and to respect the traditional norms. Nothing evoked more rage and suspicion than a foreigner who came here with "alien ideas" or (unduly) criticized America. This kind of narrow nativism, this insistence on "Americanism," burst out with great ferocity at times, even in the twentieth century. In a way, passivity and acceptance were the price minorities, as guests, were expected to pay for our national hospitality; it was the price, in other words, of the freedom and rights they enjoyed. There were even those—like prisoners—who forfeited those rights.

Modern rights, on the other hand, have a different quality. They are pushy, expansive and bold. They are less liable to forfeiture, which is another way of expressing the fact that they are more general and less liable to run afoul of old immunities and unreviewable discretions. These aspects of legal culture are corollaries of the general expectation of justice. It is impossible to tell which came first, the modern concept of equality or the modern expectation of justice; or which caused which—if indeed it makes sense to talk in these terms. They may be one and the same phenomenon.

The modern theory of equality is of course not trouble free. To say "theory of equality" suggests attitudes that are precise, systematic, and consistent. But popular ideas are complicated, imprecise, and inconsistent. Every trend, too, generates a certain backlash. Some people have to be dragged kicking and screaming into modernity. And there are genuine, unavoidable difficulties, too. Once the basic decision was made, it was possible to desegregate professional baseball, the army, and the Metropolitan Opera smoothly. It was easy to eliminate Jewish jokes on radio and TV, and even to appoint a few women, blacks, Hispanics, and handicapped people to government office. In other regards, plural equality has far tougher sledding. Radical readjustment of social arrangements is never easy. The march of women toward equality in the job market and in the family runs up against what may be the most stubborn, intractable opposition of all.

Plural equality puts a strain on old assumptions and stretches social institutions, sometimes to the breaking point. Let us take education as an example. To our weary eyes, nineteenth-century education has an almost quaint certitude, a kind of lost innocence. The old schoolbooks, the McGuffey readers and the like, were strongly didactic. They had a kind of naive self-confidence. The rules of school "were always clear"—and traditional.[40] The point of schooling was a kind of indoctrination; people took it for granted that the schoolhouse would teach prevailing morals, prevailing ideas, prevailing habits—the "American way." Education was society's device for raising the new generation in the image of the old; the new generation was supposed to be like the one that came before it, except a bit better and smarter.

Despite a certain romantic nostalgia (sometimes from high places), old-time education is dead, and few educators would be willing to revive it. To most educators, and perhaps parents, the old system was bad because it stressed rote learning, stifled creativity and individuality, and aimed to stamp out model adults like cookies from a cookie cutter. Schools today ostensibly deal with students as individuals. It is taken for granted that each child has a unique personality; the goal is not so much to assimilate the child into the dominant culture as rather to equip the child for that culture, while developing individuality and striving to achieve the child's maximum potential. Whether education really tries to reach these ends or is just mouthing slogans, and whether it can possibly succeed in these aims, or even whether these are sensible goals—all these are another matter.

Schools today are supposed to be neutral and objective. They no longer teach history from the standpoint of "us" (white, male Americans) as opposed to "them" (foreigners, black people, women, and so on) who simply never appeared on the stage. In the past, however, the goal of education, for millions of immigrant children, was assimilation. They were supposed to shed their languages, their cultures, their traditions, perhaps even their religions, and become "real" Americans.

Assimilation is still a powerful ideal, as the ferocious controversy over bilingual education suggests. But in some respects, assimilation has had to give ground to plural equality. The old ethnic traditions get more respect, both for themselves and for what they contributed to the making of America. Textbooks today are supposed to reflect various viewpoints—they must give equal time to groups that demand the right to have their story heard. Textbooks have been revised—and repeatedly—to try to satisfy various groups.[41]

Here, however, pluralism can easily run up against a stone wall. No kind of education, and no history book, can be completely neutral and objective. What is meant, or should be meant, is that the school has a duty to expose students to more than one viewpoint. Schools should look at our social and historical landscape through more than one lens; there should be a range, a band, a rainbow of viewpoints. But it is impossible to give everybody a piece of the action; there are too many actors. Nor is school going to give space or time to the American Nazi Party, or the Ku Klux Klan, or present American history as Fidel Castro would write it. But school can and should explain that many groups dwell in this house, that no single moral code deserves total dominance, that there is no single correct slant on the story. Nobody owns the American dream simply because his ancestors came over on the Mayflower.

This is difficult but possible to achieve. Schools have discarded McGuffey's Readers, and they can wring the worst chauvinism out of textbooks. As children learn to read, they see pictures of blacks as well as whites in their readers and spellers. But there are matters that cannot be reconciled. Either God made birds, bees, monkeys, lizards, woman, and man in a single week, or else they evolved as Darwin and modern biologists have it. Schools cannot fudge this question entirely. This issue erupted into conflict in the Scopes trial (1925), and continues to foment conflict to this day. This is only one example out of many. It is hard to imagine a textbook that would satisfy the millions who believe in Biblical morality; and at the same time satisfy those who assert gay pride or women's equality.

A Summary Word

The chapter began with a definition and a question. It does not close with a definitive answer. The question was: are Americans becoming more claims-conscious? Or, put another way, are there measurable, detectable changes in American legal character, over time?

What this chapter tried to do is trace certain changes in legal culture and legal behavior—those associated with the concepts of individualism and equality. Whether these changes in culture and behavior bring about, or amount to, changes in modal personality are questions that cannot be answered. Americans may or may not be more claims-conscious than they were a century ago. But it can be said that the legal context in which Americans think and live has changed, in ways that make claims-consciousness a more likely response to certain stimuli than before. At the same time, changes in substantive law increase the gains to be gotten from claims and lower the losses. New definitions of equality also redefine the kinds of claims minority groups can press in court, or in other institutions. These "minorities" include tort victims and people whose Social Security checks stop coming, as well as blacks and other more recognized minorities. Ultimately, no doubt, a culture of high expectations of justice may penetrate the marrow so thoroughly, that it does make sense to talk of personality change.

NOTES

1. For the literature in the United States, see Austin Sarat, "Studying American Legal Culture: An Assessment of Survey Research," *Law & Society Review* 11 (1977):427.

2. See, for example, David Potter, *People of Plenty: Economic Abundance and the American Character* (1954).

3. See, in general, Marc Galanter's essay, "Reading the Landscape of Disputes: What We Know and Don't Know (and Think We Know) about Our Allegedly Contentious and Litigious Society," *UCLA Law Review* 31 (1983):4.

4. Jeffrey O'Connell and Rita J. Simon, "Payment for Pain and Suffering: Who Wants What, When and Why?" *Univ. Ill. Law Forum* (1972):1.

5. Joseph G. Baldwin, *The Flush Times of Alabama and Mississippi* (1853), p. 241.

6. George B. Curtis, "The Colonial County Court, Social Forum and Legislative Precedent, Accomack County, Virginia, 1633–1639," *Va. Magazine of Hist. and Biog.* 85 (1977):274.

7. The reference, of course, is to David Riesman's book *The Lonely Crowd: A Study of the Changing American Character* (1950).

8. See Roger Lane, "Urbanization and Criminal Violence in the Nineteenth Century: Massachusetts as a Test Case," *J. Social History* 2 (1968):468; for the same process on an international scale, see Ted R. Gurr and Peter N. Grabosky, *Rogues, Rebels and Reformers: A Political History of Urban Crime and Conflict* (1976).

9. Daniel S. Smith and Michael S. Hindus, "Premarital Pregnancy in America, 1640–1971: An Overview and Interpretation," *J. Interdisciplinary History* 5 (1975):561.

10. John Philip Reid, *Law for the Elephant: Property and Social Behavior on the Overland Trail* (1980).

11. See Eric H. Monkkonen, *The Dangerous Class: Crime and Poverty in Columbus, Ohio, 1860–1885* (1975), pp. 158–162; John C. Schneider, *Detroit and the Problem of Order, 1830–1880: A Geography of Crime, Riot, and Policing* (1980).

12. 411 U.S. 677 (1973).

13. For example, Code of Va. 1849, Art. 30, ch. 103, sec. 3: ("Every person who has one-fourth part or more of Negro blood.")

14. See Norma Basch, *In the Eyes of the Law: Women, Marriage and Property in Nineteenth-Century New York* (1982); Peggy Rabkin, *Fathers to Daughters: The Legal Foundations of Female Emancipation* (1980).

15. Bryan v. Walton, 14 Ga. 185 (1853).

16. 118 U.S. 356 (1886).

17. Quoted in Lawrence M. Friedman, *A History of American Law* (1973), p. 306; see also Carl B. Swisher, *Motivation and Political Technique in the California Constitutional Convention, 1878–79* (1930), pp. 86–92.

18. Story, J., in Vidal v. Girard's Exrs., 2 How. (43 U.S.) 127, 198 (1844).

19. *Journal of the Constitutional Convention of the State of New Hampshire, December 1876*, p. 37.

20. 2 Del. [2 Harr.] 553 (1837).

21. " . . . [W]hen that distant day shall arise . . . in which the people shall forsake the faith of their forefathers for such miserable delusions, no human power can constrain them from compelling every man who lives among them to respect their feelings." Id., at 571.

22. 8 Johns. 290 (N.Y. 1811).

23. Justice Story, too, in the famous Girard will case, Vidal v. Girard's Exr's, 2 How. (43 U.S.) 127, 199 (1844) dodged the issue of the "legal effect of a devise . . . for the establishment of a school or college, for the propagation of Judaism, or Deism, or any other form of infidelity." The implication is that Story doubted whether the law could allow such a devise to be carried out.

24. Meyer v. Nebraska, 262 U.S. 390 (1923).

25. Quoted in Peter Farb, *Word Play: What Happens When People Talk* (1975), p. 63.

26. State v. Mockus, 120 Maine 84, 113 Atl. 39 (1921).

27. 9 Md. App. 270, 263 Atl. 2d 603 (1970).

28. A recent Supreme Court decision, Lynch v. Donnelly, 52 U.S. Law Week 4317 (1984) does represent something of a small chink in the wall. The Court upheld a public "Christmas display" in Pawtucket, Rhode Island, including a crèche.

29. Engel v. Vitale, 370 U.S. 421 (1962).

30. 98 U.S. 145 (1878).

31. Ibid., p. 166.

32. Ibid., p. 164.

33. 406 U.S. 205 (1972).

34. Ibid., pp. 213, 222.

35. Ibid., pp. 212, 218.

36. Frank Way and Barbara J. Burt, "Religious Marginality and the Free Exercise Clause," Am. Pol. Sci. Rev. 77 (1983):652.

37. Jackson, J., in West Va. Bd. of Education v. Barnette, 319 U.S. 624 (1943), overruling Minersville School District v. Gobitis, 310 U.S. 586 (1940).

38. Bob Jones University v. U.S., 461 U.S. —, 103 S.Ct. 2017 (1983). The university excluded blacks until 1971, excluded unmarried blacks until 1975, and even after 1975 forbade interracial dating.

39. See Mildred A. Schwartz, Trends in White Attitudes Toward Negroes (1967); Paul Burstein, "Public Opinion, Demonstrations, and the Passage of Antidiscrimination Legislation," Public Opinion Quarterly 43 (1979):157.

40. David Tyack and Elisabeth Hansot, Managers of Virtue: Public School Leadership in America, 1820–1980 (1982), p. 27.

41. See Frances FitzGerald, America Revised (1979).

7

SEXUAL BEHAVIOR AND THE LAW: A CASE IN POINT

E ARLIER CHAPTERS tried to trace changes in American legal culture over the past hundred years or so, moving toward a cluster of principles summed up in the phrase "total justice." This chapter will look at a specific area of law: control of sexual behavior. This will serve as an illustration of some of the themes of this study. In some ways, however, the growth of the law in this area seems to go against the grain. In other parts of social life, zones of immunity to law have been shrinking; but this is a tale of *new* immunity. We live in an age that is more laissez faire, as far as sexual behavior is concerned, than the nineteenth century was. In the past, little or nothing was heard of a right of privacy that protected behavior that the majority considered immoral, or intolerable in civilized society. How do we account for this apparent contradiction in trends?

Delegalization, moreover, goes far beyond sexual behavior. It is a striking feature of family law as well, most notably in divorce law. No-fault divorce, which swept the country after 1970, is a stunning setback to traditional morality as well as to the "imperial judiciary." Here is at least one corner of law where courts have *lost* some power and discretion.

It is, of course, impossible to discuss all fields of law. I will use the history of control over sexual behavior to try to resolve the paradox (delegalization in the midst of the "law explosion") and explore further the thesis of this book. This might shed light on other parts of law that affect morality—divorce, for example. But the main theme is sexual conduct.

The American legal system, like other legal systems, has always concerned itself with sexual behavior; it is the subject of a large, complicated field of law. But for most of our history, certain basic assumptions underlay the doctrines and practices. It was assumed that authority in this society (as in others) had the right, indeed the duty, to control sexual behavior. Sexual behavior was emphatically not just a matter of personal choice; it was a matter for collective choice, a matter of law.

Today it is apparent to the naked eye that this assumption no longer goes unquestioned, to say the least. Traditional legal controls are under persistent attack, and have become much weaker. Of course, there are still norms for sexual behavior that almost everybody accepts (few speak up for child molestation or rape). But many norms have recently been reshaped. Some old rules have been abolished altogether; some have been recast and redefined.

The Rise and Fall of Victimless Crime

Many people see some sort of organic connection between the "Puritan heritage" of colonial America, and modern notions of sexuality and law. There is the conventional picture of the Puritans as stern, sour people dressed in dark-colored clothes who were suspicious of intense pleasure, especially sex. Some people imagine that the spirit of the Puritans never died; that colonial "blue laws," for example, lived on, and that a tradition, descending directly from those ancient days, holds society in its bony, intolerant clutch.

Nobody would deny some connection between American tradition and legal norms of sexual behavior. Biblical religion has always been a powerful influence in the United States. Millions have always believed in the Bible as the literal word of God. The criminal codes from the very beginning expressed rules of sexual behavior that reflect religious tradition. They were not literally Biblical rules, but they were rules that corresponded to the way Americans and their religious leaders understood and interpreted the Bible.

But this does not mean that a kind of historical daisy chain links Cotton Mather to the present day. For one thing, most Americans do not "descend" from Puritans, in body or soul. The Puritan way of life is gone from religious and secular beliefs as well as practices and customs. Nobody dresses like the Puritans, or eats like them, or governs like them. Why, then, should Puritan ideas about sex be so persistent? Why should these be stronger and more durable than the rest of their ideas? What mechanism would account for this longevity? Moreover, despite what most people think, there is no direct, unbroken line of repression in the story of legal controls over sex. Many "traditional" offenses were criminalized more recently than most people think—abortion for one; and other moral offenses, such as drug addiction, also have relatively short legal histories.

The colonial attitude toward sex offenses is nonetheless quite interesting. Particularly striking was their view of what is now called "victimless crime." The phrase, of course, is relatively modern, and so is the idea. It implies that there is something wrong with punishing these acts. If there is no victim, what is the point of the punishment? The very words, then, tend to prejudge the issue. But if anybody stood up for such "victimless crimes" as fornication, adultery, or sodomy in colonial Massachusetts, they left no trace behind.

Take, for example, fornication, one of the most common of these "crimes," and a rapidly disappearing one (as a crime, not a behavior). To the clergy and magistrates who ran colonial Massachusetts, it was only natural to punish this offense. Colonial law expressed this view clearly. In the *Laws and Liberties of Massachusetts* (1648) it was stated that "if any man shall commit Fornication with any single woman, they shall be punished either by enjoyning to Marriage, or Fine, or corporall punishment, or all or any of these as the Judges . . . shall appoint most agreeable to the word of God."

The leaders of the Puritan colonies were as good as their word. Studies of court records show that fornication was perhaps the single most commonly punished crime in old New England. There are hundreds of cases on record of men and women whipped, fined, and put in the stocks for committing this offense. The load of fornication cases continued to be heavy throughout the colonial period.[1] Nor was punishment confined to New England. Christopher Burroughs and Mary Somes, of Norfolk, Virginia, were found guilty of fornication in 1641. For this offense, they had to "do penance in their parish church" on the Sabbath. They were to stand on a stool in the "middle alley" of the church dressed in white sheets, holding white wands in their hands, and repeat "after the minister such words as he shall deliver unto them before the congregation."[2] In general, more women were punished than men, especially women who were pregnant and unmarried; but on the whole it is clear that the colonies took fornication quite seriously.

The law, in colonial Massachusetts and elsewhere, forbade other forms of sexual misconduct—adultery, sodomy, and wilder variations on the general theme. In the early eighteenth century, a grand jury in Kent County, Delaware, indicted a certain James White, a boy of about fifteen, who "did seemingly Commit Buggery with a Mare of Isack Freeland in Mr. Frenches Pasture" (White denied actually doing the deed; Thomas French, White said, interrupted him before he could get around to his crime).[3]

These various offenses were not really victimless, as contemporaries saw it. They harmed society as a whole and were offenses against God's law. They could destroy a society from within; such abominations, after all, led God to strike down Sodom and Gomorrah with fiery destruction. Sin and crime, in general, were not sharply distinguished in seventeenth-century thought. The *Laws and Liberties* refers to the "word of God" as a source of law—perhaps the most important source. Biblical passages were cited in support of laws that called for capital punishment. The leaders of society were deeply religious men. Religion was to them the very cornerstone of society, its reason for being, its justification on earth. They made no great distinction between divine laws and the laws that should govern men.

The seventeenth-century settlements were tiny places, too, where everybody knew everybody else, and everybody's business was more or less public. For a community to enforce laws against (say) fornication, there are at least two prerequisites: first, the leaders of the community, backed by respectable opinion, must feel strongly that fornication *should* be punished; second, there has to be some way to ferret out sinners and punish them for their acts.

Colonial Massachusetts had both of these requirements. Leading opinion—which no doubt percolated rather far down into society—condemned sex before marriage, sex after marriage but with the wrong partner, and all other forms of sexual behavior that the Bible or tradition condemned. Moreover, in small, gossipy, inbred communities, there was a good chance that those who stumbled would be caught in their sin. There is no way to know how many people sinned and got away with it; but hundreds did not. The pregnant servant girl was condemned by the shape of her body; faced with the inescapable truth, she was likely to expose her partner as well.

But the system of neighborhood control had weaknesses even in the seventeenth century,[4] and by 1800 these were glaringly obvious. Communities grew in size; there were towns like Boston and New York filled with newcomers, sailors, taverns, and vice. On the whole, people in this country were exceptionally mobile. There was heavy immigration; even among native-born Americans, there was constant coming and going as people left their home villages to settle in new places. America was still a religious society—waves of religious enthusiasm swept over the country from time to time—but the hold of the clergy on society had definitely weakened, compared to (say) seventeenth-century Massachusetts. The climate of opinion changed, as far as one can tell, along with the structural conditions needed to enforce laws against "crimes" like fornication.

The legal records show the decline and fall of fornication as a punishable crime. There is some squabbling among scholars about when the change took place; it had certainly happened by about 1800. William Nelson reports that of 2,784 criminal prosecutions between 1760 and 1774 in Superior and General Sessions courts of colonial Massachusetts, no less than 1,074, or 38 percent, were for sexual offenses; 95 percent of these were for fornication. By way of contrast, there were only 355 prosecutions for property offenses.[5] By 1800, however, fornication cases had dropped to almost nothing.

Some scholars feel the essential change took place earlier. Nelson's

own figures show that late-eighteenth-century prosecutions were almost always cases where a child had been born out of wedlock. "Pure"
fornication prosecutions were already uncommon.[6] In any event, what
replaced fornication—and blasphemy, idleness, and nonattendance at
church—in the annals of criminal justice, in the early nineteenth
century, was property crime: theft, in its various forms. This was by a
huge margin the most commonly punished crime. This was also true
in England; over 90 percent of the prosecutions for serious crimes in
the central criminal courts of London, in some years, were for theft
and related crimes.[7]

Morals offenses were not, on the whole, wiped off the statute books.
But there were, it seems, few arrests and convictions. In the course of
the nineteenth century, legal doctrine changed subtly, and statutes
were reworded in ways that suggest changes in legal culture. Of course,
the physical problem of catching sex offenders was great in communities without modern police forces and with people coming and
going all the time. Colonial leaders had condemned fornication and
adultery as inherently immoral acts: they were offenses against society
because they offended God. Now the stress shifted to public rather
than private morality—to the time, manner, and mode of commission. The offense was redefined as a crime against public sentiment,
against public morality. The essential evil was defiance of an official
moral code.

Take, for example, the (largely unenforced) laws against adultery. In
Alabama, it was a misdemeanor for any man and woman to "live
together in adultery or fornication."[8] In Indiana and other states, the
statute condemned "open and notorious adultery," which meant that
"occasional illicit intercourse" was not an offense at all.[9] The problem
was not sin in itself, but the flaunting of sin; not private vice, but vice
practiced in such a way as to offend the public, or to attack the official
morality. What happened behind closed doors, quietly and discreetly,
was left alone, either because not much could be done about it, or
(more likely) because people accepted it as inevitable and discounted
its danger to society.

This double standard, if you will, appears elsewhere in the law. It is
found, for example, in the legal attitude toward prostitution. Prostitution was a feature of urban life in America, as it was in other countries.
There was a brothel in Boston as early as the 1650s.[10] Prostitution was

always illegal in the United States and there were sporadic attempts to get rid of it altogether. In the eighteenth and nineteenth centuries, there were eruptions of so-called whorehouse riots; mobs pillaged and burned brothels in Boston, New York, St. Louis, Chicago, and Detroit, among other cities.[11]

Despite such signs of violent disapproval, most people seemed to accept prostitution, or at least take it as inevitable. (There were also, of course, great numbers of men who *patronized* prostitutes; their influence may have been felt on the law in some quiet way.) It is almost as if a peculiarly Victorian compromise had been worked out, roughly parallel to the "compromise" inherent in statutes against open and notorious adultery. Prostitution would continue to be illegal. It would not be openly legitimated. But it could operate with a certain immunity so long as it obeyed rules of decorum, order, and ecology—so long as it stayed in its place.

That place was the so-called red-light district. Every big city had one. Police ignored what went on in these districts, or accepted bribes to let the districts alone. In New York in 1864, according to one account, there were 599 houses of prostitution "of all grades," and 2,123 prostitutes. "People who keep houses of ill-repute have no motive to keep their trade . . . a secret"; the police shut their eyes to these houses, unless "they are noisy, disturb the peace, or become a public nuisance. . . . All the public houses . . . are known to the authorities."[12]

This was not true only of New York. Indeed, in some cities, ordinances spelled out the boundaries of red-light districts—though legally such places could not exist. This was, for example, the situation in New Orleans; by ordinance, no "public prostitute or woman notoriously abandoned to lewdness" was allowed to "live or sleep" outside the district. At least one citizen brought a lawsuit to protest against this ordinance. (His own house was in the district and therefore in danger of attracting these "lewd" women.) The case reached the Supreme Court of the United States in 1900, but the Court refused to interfere.[13] In an interesting Texas case (1890), a woman named Emilia Garza had been fined for disobeying a San Antonio ordinance, which levied a $500 license fee on every "bawdy-house." The appeal court threw out her conviction, on the grounds that San Antonio had no power to require such a license; Texas law made Ms. Garza's business totally illegal.[14]

The situation in Chicago in the early twentieth century was even more bizarre. State law forbade prostitution and houses of ill-fame; so did the municipal code of Chicago. Yet the police recognized a definite red-light district. In 1910, the Department even issued "Rules Governing the Regulation of Vice." For example, no "house of ill-fame" was permitted outside of the "restricted district," or "within two blocks of any school, church, hospital or public institution, or upon any street car line." The police rules covered other matters: for example, they outlawed "swinging doors that permit of easy access" to the houses, or allowed "a view of the interior from the street." There were also to be no "short skirts, transparent gowns or other improper attire," in "parlors, or public rooms." Nor did the rules allow "conspicuous" signs or "devices," "indicative of the character of any premises occupied by a house of ill-repute."[15]

This Victorian compromise is an interesting, and in some ways puzzling, phenomenon. To the modern nose, it smells of hypocrisy and class bias. The law was always tougher on the common street-walker than on genteel houses that catered to prosperous men. But underneath the contradictory surface lurked an implicit theory of social control. It was as if people recognized that they could not, realistically, get rid of vice, drunkenness, and so on; perhaps there was no real will to do so. What was needed was not abolition but control. One guarantee of morality was to insist that official standards must be maintained at an adequate level, and to tolerate some vice, perhaps as a safety valve, so long as it was discreet, kept in its place, and above all, did not openly challenge official norms.

Why would such a policy work? What could it accomplish? It would not work by itself, that was clear. But official morality could strengthen other sources of living morality: the church, the family, the school. All of these institutions, acting in concert, worked to socialize people into society; they worked to maintain norms needed for discipline and order. They helped bring up children with the right outlook and habits; helped to produce the model nineteenth-century human: the hard-working, moral citizen.

The nineteenth century, in other words, relied on self-control, which it tried to support through legal institutions, as well as other social processes. The enforcement power of law was used rather sparingly; law was unnecessary for most people, who were, after all, quite successful in controlling themselves. The problem with formal law was that it was not very effective, in this sphere of life at least. Meanwhile, the real system, the living law, allowed vice to continue but, in effect, raised its price. Prostitution posed less of a threat to official norms if it was illegal but controlled, than if it was totally legalized—by a licensing system, for example. A modern analogy is highway speeding. Speeding is as common as dirt, but it is quite illegal. The laws against it are enforced, up to a point. There is never enough enforcement to stamp out speeding, and it is clear that people do not want to stamp it out. Most people are speeders themselves, from time to time. There is enough enforcement, however, to maintain some sort of control. To get rid of all limits would set off an explosion of speeding, and perhaps lead to chaos on the roads.

Law, of course, has always had a definite role to play in keeping the normative system going. It punishes blatant offenses, those that strike at the code of morality itself; and it represents, in vivid and official form, the code that carries the imprimatur of state and society. Law is, in other words, not simply a force machine. It also expresses moral hegemony. It has the sole franchise on official norms. It holds the monopoly of legitimate violence, and it expresses what was intended to be a monopoly of legitimacy itself.

This does not mean, of course, that law was the only or main support for a system of personal self-control. Science itself (or pseudo-science) taught the same lessons. The person who overindulged (in drink, sex, vice) ran a grave risk of ruining his health and his life. Sex was believed to be toxic in large doses. It was associated with the "animal" part of human nature; it was "characteristic of a brutal, less highly organized being."[16] Civilized people had to bring it under control. A prominent doctor, in the early part of this century, put it this way: "the development of the mental faculties lessens very materially the sexual impulse, that impulse being always strongest in races of the lowest order of intelligence."[17] Law, science, official morality, education, religion—these systems joined in an interlocking net of norms that pointed in the same direction and gave out the same message. There were always dissenters and exceptions, but the central tendency was brutally clear.

Yet, beginning about 1870, there were creaking noises and break-downs in the machinery; the Victorian compromise, it seems, was not working very well. In the late nineteenth century, it began to break down dramatically. I am not necessarily talking about behavior (that is pretty much unknown), but about the ability of the "compromise" to satisfy both sides to the bargain. Most notably, moral reformers, never completely satisfied, refused to accept old, comfortable arrangements. They began to demand more teeth in the moral code.

An early sign, in the 1870s, was the rise of societies "for the suppression of vice." One Boston organization, later called the Watch and Ward Society, became particularly famous. In 1873, Congress passed the so-called Comstock law, which tightened the rules against mailing "obscene, lewd, or lascivious" books and pictures. Included was a ban on mailing any "article or thing designed for the prevention of conception or procuring of abortion."[18] In this period, too, abortion first became a crime, in most jurisdictions. Between 1860 and 1880 states and territories passed some forty antiabortion statutes. Many were first-time statutes; they entered what had been largely a legal void.[19]

The statutory attack on victimless crime and immoral behavior continued into the twentieth century. In 1895, Congress outlawed the sale of lottery tickets across state lines, and lotteries went underground for the next seventy years.[20] The antilottery law was in some ways a radical extension of the power of Congress to regulate interstate commerce. In 1910, Congress went even further, in the Mann Act.[21] This famous law came up out of a background of hysteria over "white slavery." The idea was that predatory, vicious men trapped innocent girls, dragged them into the big cities, and forced them to become prostitutes. There they lived a life of degradation from which they could never escape.[22]

Originally, the campaign against "white slavery" emphasized keeping foreign prostitutes out of the country. But the problem, as contemporaries saw it, was far more general and severe. The text of the law, as enacted, was bold and sweeping. Under the Mann Act, it was a crime to "transport" any woman or girl across state lines "for the purpose of prostitution or debauchery, or for any other immoral purpose." In subsequent cases, the Supreme Court read the words "immoral purpose" very broadly.[23] The Court refused, in particular, to limit the statute to "commercialized" vice. The Mann Act is still on the books today, though the zeal to enforce it has probably cooled off considerably, and standards of "debauchery" have changed greatly over the years.

The Mann Act, however, was only one of many signs that the cold war against vice was heating up. Another symptom was the so-called red-light abatement movement, which flourished around the time of the First World War. The aim of this movement was to end the comfortable compromises which protected the red-light districts. The movement rejected out of hand the European way of dealing with the "social evil" (prostitution) through regulation and licensing, in the interests of health. There had been a few sporadic attempts at regulation in this country—notably in St. Louis, Missouri, between 1872 and 1874—but the righteous expressed their wrath, and these attempts were stamped out.[24]

The red-light abatement movement began in wide-open Chicago. An evangelist, Rodney Smith (sometimes called "Gypsy"), led a band of 12,000 marchers through the red-light district on 22nd Street in October 1909. A meeting in January 1910 at the Central YMCA Building in Chicago discussed the "social evil"; clergymen from 600 churches attended. They demanded a vice commission to study and deal with the problem. The commission was appointed; in 1911 it issued its well-known report on the "Social Evil in Chicago."[25]

The commission wanted to do away with "restricted districts," where by "custom" the laws against vice did not penetrate. Great crowds demanded action to carry out this program. This time, the police responded. All over the country, cities issued vice reports; from New York to Honolulu, angry citizens demanded an end to the red-light districts. Some states passed draconian laws to get rid of prostitution. Under the Michigan law, for example, any private citizen could go to court to abate a disorderly house, as a "nuisance."[26] This took the matter out of the hands of the police and robbed the payoff (at least in theory) of some of its potency.

Intense public pressure always has an effect on police and local politicians. In 1917, the police blockaded the famous Barbary Coast in San Francisco. They closed 83 brothels and drove 1,073 women out of the neighborhood.[27] In this period, too, Storyville, the famous New Orleans district, was put out of business. All over the country, red-light districts felt the effects of the movement.

What effect all this had on vice itself is another question. Walter Lippmann sneered at the battle against the "Tenderloin." It only succeeded (he said) in "sprinkling the Tenderloin through the whole city."[28] This was certainly true. But still, the new, more intense desire to do something about vice was significant. In part, it was a reaction to a heightened sense of physical danger: fear of venereal disease, for example, and its effect on population, in an age before the discovery of antibiotics. Syphilis destroyed the lives of thousands of men and women, many of them innocent victims ("debauched" husbands infected their wives and children). But there was more to the story. The general struggle against immorality spilled over into areas where to our way of thinking there was no physical danger. Many thinkers of the late nineteenth century expanded their notion of the threat to health to include the (assumed) effects of vice on the health of society—on the future of "the race"; on the very fabric of society. Hence the general war on immorality.

At this time, too, drug addiction became a crime. This had not been the case in the nineteenth century. Nobody thought addiction (to opium, for example) was a good idea, but it was not against the law. Early drug laws were not directed against addiction as such, but against the evil places where people went to buy or use the drugs. The first California laws and ordinances were against "opium dens." The California Penal Code, in 1881, made it a misdemeanor to operate a "place where opium . . . is sold or given away, to be smoked at such place"; it was also a crime to "resort" to an opium den.[29]

The California campaign against opium was in many ways a thinly disguised campaign against the Chinese. Similarly, the later laws against marijuana were colored by prejudice against Mexican-Americans. In general, nineteenth-century drug legislation, such as it was, was unusually feeble. A few of these laws and ordinances began to treat drugs as what would now be called controlled substances. An 1890 ordinance of Oakland, California, which applied to morphine and cocaine as well as opium, required a doctor's prescription.[30] Similarly, under an Illinois law (1897) cocaine was to be sold by druggists, and only "upon the written prescription of a licensed physician or licensed dentist."[31]

In 1914, Congress took a major step, and passed the so-called Harrison Act.[32] This law, too, restricted the sale of narcotics without a doctor's prescription. In practice, the law came to mean a flat prohibition on the sale of narcotics, helped along by a fateful reading of the act by the Supreme Court in *Webb* v. *U.S.* (1919).[33] A doctor named Webb, in Memphis, Tennessee, prescribed morphine for addicts "in such quantities as desired for the sake of continuing their accustomed use." A druggist named Goldbaum regularly filled these prescriptions. Webb and Goldbaum were charged with violating the Harrison Act. The statute allowed the use of drugs for "medical" purposes. But the court thought it crystal clear that a maintenance dose given to an addict was not a medical use. To say it was would be "so plain a perversion of meaning that no discussion . . . is required." From that point on, the addict stood outside the law.

Some states went so far as to criminalize sale of cigarettes— Arkansas in 1907, for example.[34] But the jewel in the crown of the movement against vice was, unquestionably, the triumphant campaign against liquor. Prohibition began in 1919, when the Eighteenth Amendment was ratified. The amendment flatly prohibited the "manufacture, sale, or transportation of intoxicating liquors" within the United States. Congress passed a strong enforcement act; many states enacted little Prohibitions of their own.

Prohibition turned into a national nightmare. It collapsed by the early 1930s. But this takes nothing away from the dazzling victory of the temperance movement. There had always been strong temperance forces in American history, and there had been important local victories. But a total national ban on alcohol was a stunning turn of events.

There is overwhelming evidence, then, of an upsurge of interest in crimes against morality between 1870 and 1920, and a serious attempt to suppress vice and debauchery, as conventionally defined. Whether all this activity had much effect beyond the pages of statute books is another question. Some of these laws were unquestionably more effective than others. Prohibition undoubtedly had an impact. There was massive evasion and violation, and the bad side effects probably far outweighed the direct effects, some of which were fairly desirable. Prohibition no doubt influenced the style, manner, and amount of drinking in the country. Prohibition was a political disaster; but alcoholism declined; and the thousands who went to jail or paid fines could certainly testify that Prohibition was no "dead letter," despite leaks and holes in enforcement.[35]

There is some reason, too, to believe that the police made more arrests for morals offenses in this period than had been true in earlier years. The numbers overall were surely small. In Oakland, California,

arrests for serious morals charges (gambling and drunkenness aside) ran
to less than 1 percent of arrests between 1872 and 1910. Few people
were ever prosecuted for sodomy, adultery, and the like. Only 5 percent of all felony prosecutions were for crimes against morality.[36]
There was perhaps a good deal of local variation. One authority
claimed that Washington, D.C. and Cincinnati, in 1916, prosecuted
something like 1,000 cases of fornication and 131 cases of adultery; in
the same year New York City prosecuted only 10 cases of adultery; in
Atlanta and Savannah, Georgia, 70 persons were arrested for adultery,
none for fornication.[37]

The records of Alameda County, California, do show some prosecutions for statutory rape—sexual relations with a girl below the "age
of consent." Here too the legislature showed heightened interest after
1870. Originally, in California, the age of consent was ten, which was
the so-called common-law age (the age that governed if there was no
statute). This meant that it was no crime—or at least not rape—to
have sex with a girl of eleven or older. The age of consent was then
raised to fourteen; to sixteen in 1897; and finally, in 1913, the age of
consent became eighteen. This meant that sex with a seventeen-year-
old girl, even a willing one, even a prostitute, was a serious crime in
California—even if the male was himself sixteen or seventeen. Thus
California had criminalized, on paper at least, a tremendous range of
sexual behavior, which had not been taken seriously before.[38]

California was not alone in tinkering with the age of consent. New
York, too, started out with the common-law age (ten); by 1895, New
York had fixed eighteen as the age of consent for some kinds of statutory rape. Not all states went this far: Mississippi never got past twelve,
and Georgia stopped at fourteen.[39] But in every state, the direction of
change was the same: the common-law age was deemed too young and
was replaced by a higher age. The same thing happened in England.[40]

What lay behind the tremendous drive against immorality that
changed so many features of the law after 1870? Why did the Victorian
compromise break down? Why did respectable society feel so threatened by vice? There is, of course, no single answer. In part, science
itself seemed to show the dangers of vice. The wages of sin were less
theological than before, and more medical and concrete. Prostitution
and promiscuity became grave problems of public health. Drug addiction too began to seem exceedingly dangerous. Heroin did not even

exist until 1898; Coca-Cola contained cocaine until 1903; opium was an ingredient in many patent medicines. Warning bells were slow to sound, but when they did, the legislatures responded.

But these are only partial explanations, and ultimately fail to account for the whole of the story or to explain why the campaign against vice became so vehement. If prostitution and venereal disease were truly medical problems, then why not use the system of licensing and health inspection? Nor does the sense of physical danger explain the urge to tighten the screws against sexuality among young people. As I remarked, there was a feeling that (in the broad sense) the general health of society was at risk. And one sees a decline in the faith that traditional institutions, together with self-control, were strong enough to keep the restless human spirit within proper bounds.

Some authors, notably Joseph Gusfield, have linked the outburst of moral crusades with changes in American demography. On one side stood the old-line Protestants; on the other, endless human waves of new immigrants, Catholics and Jews for the most part, from southern and eastern Europe. There was a serious clash of norms; and Prohibition (this was Gusfield's subject) was the last-ditch, desperate attempt of old-line WASPs to impose their values, at least symbolically, on the country at large. Prohibition was an example of "coercive reform," and coercive reform is itself a "reaction to a sense of declining dominance."[41]

The thesis is an attractive one. As Gusfield sees it, the dangers to society were not so much physical as moral. Prohibition was not a reaction to the spread of drunkenness. If anything people were drinking less as the country became more "civilized." The crisis was moral and symbolic: the new immigrants did not accept the old values; they did not accept their "place" in society. They did not bow down to the old rulers of America; and they ultimately demanded, not only classic American rights, but also legitimacy. They wanted recognition of their way of life; they felt their norms and practices were as valid, as legitimate, as the norms and practices of old-line Americans.

The Gusfield thesis can thus be broadened to include, not just Catholics and Jews from eastern and southern Europe, but all the submerged minorities—blacks, women, gays, ethnics, Jehovah's Witnesses, radicals, the handicapped, and so on. All of them changed their attitude toward majority culture. They no longer accepted equality in its bounded, nineteenth-century version; they reformulated the concept along the lines of plural equality. The morals campaign was thus a reaction, a form of resistance, to the threat to the ancient order—the old system of moral hegemony.

Each group, to be sure, fought the battle in its own way. The battle is often described as "symbolic"; this is illuminating, but also misleading. It does not do full justice to the civil rights movement to describe it in those terms. Blacks and their allies were not mainly arguing over symbols. They wanted rights, plain, old-fashioned rights of the most basic type. The turn of the century was, in many ways, a dark and bloody period in race relations. The mass of the black population was poor, ignorant, voteless, and landless. A form of peonage held black laborers in its grip.[42] Jim Crow kept blacks in their place, and the lynch mob enforced the Southern "code." Most Southern blacks were little better than serfs. A thicket of laws and practices bound them to a life of hard work, poverty, and oppression. Their needs were desperate and fundamental. But in the course of time, all the minorities began to claim more than substance; they began to demand legitimacy; they wanted equal validation. They insisted that the house of America—to use this metaphor once again—was owned in common, and was not, as had been assumed, the house of the WASPs, with some tolerated visitors and tenants. Why this was so important is a complex question, but there are at least two obvious answers. In the first place, symbolic tools have instrumental uses, especially in a country committed formally to equal rights. In the second place, human beings want dignity as well as bread; honor alongside cash.

In the second third of the twentieth century, the balance shifted toward plural equality, and the civil rights movement began to make marvelous progress. At the same time, attitudes toward sexual norms changed dramatically. This too had a deep effect on law. The nineteenth century believed that control and repression were moral goods; they were also essential to health. Libertines paid a terrible price for their pleasures. Sex was dangerous, except in small doses. Only the moderate man or woman, the man or woman of the golden mean, was civilized—and safe.

These ideas helped legitimate the old moral code, which was the only code recognized officially. At first, people accepted the code because it was God's word; later on, science confirmed their beliefs.

Science—today it has been unmasked as pseudoscience—seemed to confirm that white people were superior to other races.[43] It confirmed that moderation was better for body and soul than debauchery. But as the fight for plural equality continued, science did an about-face. It recanted on the subject of race, and it changed its attitudes toward sex. The Kinsey report (published in the late 1940s)[44] was profoundly destructive of conventional moral order—and was meant to be. The Kinsey report claimed to strip away the conspiracy of sexual silence. It showed tremendous variety and vitality in sexual life. It argued that "deviance" was common as dirt, and should not be treated as criminal, at least for consenting adults. There was, at first, a tremendous cry of horror and alarm. But the report has outlasted and outgunned its critics.

Contemporary ideas about sexual morality have, in many ways, turned older notions inside out. Repression now is felt to be the danger—excessive control, not excessive license. A vigorous sex life is good for you; suppression of desire poses risks to body and soul. Sex is a basic drive, a fundamental force. A person's sexuality must find expression. You cannot squash sexuality without harming your personality. When the sexual drive does not find outlets one way, it gets them in another, perhaps neurotically. Basically, too, there is no such thing as too much sex. There are natural limits to performance; these are the only ones people need. A person who overeats can become obese; there is no equivalent consequence for sex. These are the current clichés.

There have been so many changes in attitudes toward sex in the past decades that people routinely speak of a "sexual revolution." This may be (some say) more talk than action. But even so it is crucial talk; it has a tremendous effect on official norms and the laws that reflect them. In some ways, the "revolution" is a counterattack; it responds to the movement that began in the 1870s, the attack of the righteous.

This counterattack has had spectacular success. The Supreme Court (as has often been the case in our times) took up a position at the head of the army. In 1965, the court struck down a Connecticut law against birth control,[45] a living fossil by then. In 1973 came Roe v. Wade,[46] which overturned all existing laws against abortion. No legal decision in modern times has been as controversial, but the core of Roe v. Wade has held firm for more than a decade.[47]

Legislatures also have been active in the counterattack. Some states have decriminalized most forms of the "crime against nature." Most states have stopped actively persecuting homosexual behavior among adults. Many victimless crimes have been swept off the books. Fornication is no longer criminal in many states.

Cohabitation, too, has become a way of life, accepted in ways that once would have shocked respectable society. In many circles (of course not all), nobody blinks an eye at unmarried couples who live together, whose irregular status is "open and notorious." Cohabitation also has some legal legitimacy. *Marvin* v. *Marvin* (1976)[48] is a well-known case in point. Cohabitation is no longer a "meretricious relationship," outside the pale; it is even a basis for property rights. A trend in the case-law heads in this direction, running powerful and clear.

More and more people, in other words, insist on freedom to carve out their own way of life, their own brand of sexuality, their own personal ethos. Obviously, there are outer limits. Absolute freedom to choose is impossible in any organized society. People live in a social context; a completely self-chosen life is as impossible as life underwater. But there is an increase in the range of choice; instead of one legitimate option, there are five, ten, perhaps twenty. The options are not, for the most part, behavioral novelties—there have always been gays and cohabiters. What is new is the demand for legitimacy, the demand that society accept the options as just as good, as valid, as the historical options, which were acceptable because they stemmed from the one true and proper moral code.

This development, then, is *not* inconsistent with those changes in legal culture described in Part I. They are a part of a single story. Reduction of uncertainty and the due process revolution have had a powerful effect on these demands for legitimacy. This is what the rise of plural equality means. The ordinary person is not a moral hero. If nonconformity means losing a job, home, position, without compensation, without a social "safety net," without any recourse, a nonconformist thinks twice before "coming out of the closet," or expressing off-beat political beliefs, or following the dictates of some tiny sect. Reduction of uncertainty and the rise of due process, themselves interconnected, created a cultural climate in which suppressed desires for legitimacy were able to rise to the surface. It is easier to be a dissenter in the United States than in a country where dissenters are tortured and shot. And it is easier to be a dissenter with tenure than a dissenter without.

Earlier on, I spoke about new superprinciples, based on norms developing within the legal culture: the general expectation of justice, and the general expectation of recompense. Changes in legal character flow from these changes in two obvious ways. First, a general expectation of justice means that people expect to be treated—by government, other people, and institutions—as valid, total human beings; they expect to be assessed and respected as unique individuals. Justice (as now understood) means ignoring one's race or religion, and allowing nonconforming life choices, within certain limits of tolerance. Second, people expect to reach freely chosen goals and freely chosen pleasures; they expect, to put it more pretentiously, full development of their selves. Of course, there are obstacles and barriers, from human or natural causes. But people expect a decent chance to overcome these obstacles. If calamity strikes, somebody should make amends, through money damages or other forms of compensation.

The goal of training, education, and socialization is to develop the self to its fullest power—not to produce "conformists" who obey authority blindly. Rather, the goal is people who freely choose the way that is best for them, from a market-basket of alternatives. (Whether this is realistic or not, whether it accurately describes life in America, or anywhere, is not the issue: the issue is popular beliefs and speculations.) Alternatives include sexual choices, too. There was, in a sense, always a range of choices; a lot of behavior was illegal, but common nonetheless. Prostitutes, after all, had customers. But many choices were victims of the Victorian compromise; they were relegated to illegitimacy, they were penalized in this or some other way; they were forced to live in a shadowy underground world. Modern legal culture exalts the self, and insists on its right to emerge from some of these shadows.

Modern legal culture, then, resolves the paradox this chapter began with: that an age which heaps rule on top of rule also deregulates sexual behavior. Sexual life is radically free from legal control, in comparison to the past and to most historical societies. The paradox, then, is no paradox at all. Modern society does not value rules for their own sake. The law reflects the norms and values of society; today, norms of total justice permeate the law. They produce more regulation here, less regulation there. To make total justice a living reality takes more rules for medical malpractice, for example, but fewer rules for fornication.

NOTES

1. See William E. Nelson, *Americanization of the Common Law: The Impact of Legal Change on Massachusetts Society, 1760–1830* (1975), p. 37; Hendrik Hartog, "The Public Law of a County Court: Judicial Government in Eighteenth Century Massachusetts," *Am. J. Legal Hist.* 20 (1976): 282, 299ff.

2. A. Scott, *Criminal Law in Colonial Virginia* (1930), p. 277.

3. Leon deValinger, Jr., ed., *Court Records of Kent County, Delaware, 1680–1705* (1959), p. 279. The *Laws and Liberties of Massachusetts* (1648) asserts that if "any man lyeth with mankinde as he lieth with a woman," both have "committed abomination," and should be "put to death."

4. See David T. Konig, *Law and Society in Puritan Massachusetts: Essex County 1629–1692* (1979), pp. 126–130.

5. William Nelson, *Americanization of the Common Law*, p. 37. Nelson also studied Plymouth County and found a high rate of prosecution for fornication there too in the eighteenth century. William E. Nelson, *Dispute and Conflict Resolution in Plymouth County, Massachusetts, 1725–1825* (1981), p. 23. Churches also disciplined their members for offenses like fornication (ibid., pp. 26–28).

6. See Hartog, "The Public Law of a County Court," pp. 299–308.

7. Lawrence M. Friedman, "The Devil Is Not Dead: Exploring the History of Criminal Justice," *Georgia Law Rev.* 11 (1977):257, 262–265.

8. See Collins v. State, 14 Ala. 608 (1848).

9. Wright v. State, 5 Blackf. [Ind.] 358 (1840).

10. Darrett B. Rutman, *Winthrop's Boston: A Portrait of a Puritan Town, 1630–1649* (1965), p. 242.

11. Mark T. Connelly, *The Response to Prostitution in the Progressive Era* (1980), p. 4; on Detroit, John C. Schneider, *Detroit and the Problem of Order, 1830–1880: A Geography of Crime, Riot, and Policing* (1980).

12. Matthew Hale Smith, *Sunshine and Shadow in New York* (1880), p. 371.

13. L'Hote v. New Orleans, 177 U.S. 587 (1900).

14. In re Garza, 28 Tex. App. 381 (1890).

15. Vice Commission of Chicago, *The Social Evil in Chicago* (1911), p. 329.

16. Charles E. Rosenberg, *No Other Gods: On Science and American Social Thought* (1976), p. 131.

17. J. Richardson Parke, *Human Sexuality*, 4th ed. (1909), p. 103.

18. Paul S. Boyer, *Purity in Print: Book Censorship in America* (1968).

19. James C. Mohr, *Abortion in America* (1978), p. 200.

20. 28 Stats. 963 (Act of 2 March, 1895), ch. 191; J. Ezell, *Fortune's Merry Wheel: the Lottery in America* (1960).

21. 36 Stats. 825 (Act of June 25, 1910).

22. On the reality of the problem of white slavery, see Ruth Rosen, *The Lost Sisterhood: Prostitution in America, 1900–1918* (1982).

23. Caminetti v. United States, 242 U.S. 470 (1917).

24. See John S. Haller and Robin M. Haller, *The Physician and Sexuality in Victorian America* (1974), pp. 242–244. Prostitution is legal in certain counties in Nevada, however.

25. Vice Commission of Chicago, *The Social Evil in Chicago* (1911).

26. Laws Mich. 1915, No. 272, p. 481.

27. Herbert Asbury, *The Barbary Coast: An Informal History of the San Francisco Underworld* (1933), pp. 312–313.

28. Quoted in Connelly, *The Response to Prostitution*, p. 109; see also Rosen, *The Lost Sisterhood*, p. 170.

29. Cal. Penal Code, sec. 307; see In re Sic, 73 Cal. 149, 14 Pac. 405 (1887).

30. Ord. no. 1214 (1890).

31. Laws Ill. 1897, p. 138; see, in general, Troy Duster, *The Legislation of Morality* (1970); and David F. Musto, *The American Disease: Origins of Narcotics Control* (1973).

32. 38 Stat. 785 (Act of Dec. 17, 1914).

33. 249 U.S. 96 (1919).

34. Acts Ark. 1907, no. 55, p. 134.

35. See J. C. Burnham, "New Perspectives on the Prohibition 'Experiment' of the 1920's," *Journal of Social History* 2 (1968):58.

36. Lawrence M. Friedman and Robert V. Percival, *The Roots of Justice: Crime and Punishment in Alameda County, California, 1870–1910* (1981), pp. 90–91, 136–137.

37. Howard B. Woolston, *Prostitution in the United States, Prior to the Entrance of the United States into the World War* (1921), pp. 229–230.

38. The California statute, Cal. Penal Code, sec. 261.5, figured in an important sex-discrimination case, Michael M. v. Superior Court, 450 U.S. 464 (1981). Michael M., the defendant was seventeen-and-a-half years old. He was charged with violating the statute. His partner was a girl one year younger than Michael. The issue was whether the statute violated the equal protection clause of the Fourteenth Amendment, in that it "makes men alone criminally liable for the act of sexual intercourse." The Court upheld the conviction, and the statute, six to three.

39. Laws N.Y. 1895, ch. 460; Laws Miss. 1908, ch. 171; Laws Ga. 1918, ch. 259.

40. For the background of the English law of 1885, 48 and 49 Vict. ch. 69, sec. 5, raising the age of consent to sixteen, see Ann Stafford, *The Age of Consent* (1964). A statute of 12 and 13 Geo. V, ch. 56, sec. 2, made explicit that it was no defense that there was "consent" to the "act of indecency."

41. Joseph Gusfield, *Symbolic Crusade: Status Politics and the American Temperance Movement* (1963), p. 87.

42. See Pete Daniel, *The Shadow of Slavery: Peonage in the South, 1901–1969* (1972).

43. See Stephen J. Gould, *The Mismeasure of Man* (1981).

44. Alfred C. Kinsey et al., *Sexual Behavior in the Human Male* (1948).

45. Griswold v. Connecticut, 381 U.S. 479 (1965).

46. 410 U.S. 113 (1973).

47. See Gilbert Y. Steiner, ed., *The Abortion Dispute and the American System* (1983) for an overview of the law and politics of the abortion dispute since *Roe v. Wade*.

48. 18 Cal. 3d 660, 557 P. 2d 106, 134 Cal. R. 815 (1976).

8

AN ASSESSMENT

T HE ARGUMENT of this book is that legal culture and legal character have been moving in a single direction, toward what I have called total justice. Total justice is a social norm; it is also, more and more, a working principle transforming legal and social institutions. Its fingerprints are all over—tort law; labor law; the law of landlord and tenant; the expansive world of constitutional law; the due process revolution; the behavior of large institutions; the regulation (or nonregulation) of aspects of private life. Whether on the whole these developments are good or bad is another issue. Since we are all prisoners of context, changes in our world often seem natural, inevitable, or progressive, and we never even question them. To other people, who are bound to the past for one reason or another, the same developments may look unnatural or regressive; they may look like decay or a weakening of the spirit, or even the devil at work.

I leave the question of good or bad open. The tone here has been mainly descriptive. I have tried to tell a story about legal change and legal culture and to offer some explanations for what has taken place. Still, the questions asked here about the legal system were not random questions; they were not asked out of idle curiosity, and they did not come out of the blue. They were questions with a point. They had theoretical interest. They were also directly relevant to policy issues, to current debate.

I began by referring to the clamor in the press and among jurists about legal excess: misuses and overextension of law. I tried to clear away some clouds that surround this issue, and explain why this society uses legal tools to reach certain goals and fill certain needs. There is risk in talking about "society" reaching out to "the legal system," as if there were an entity called "society" that is clearly separated from an entity called "the legal system." But the basic point seems sound. We see all around us the use of these legal tools; they are convenient, they work, and they carry the label of law.

Very little has been said here about the process of transforming attitudes—the legal culture—into structures of law, or the process of choosing which legal tools to use, or how those tools are shaped, and the institutional forms they take. The process is certainly not automatic. Existing structures of law and government, at least in the short run, exert a powerful influence on the way demands and attitudes become concrete. Political organization is an essential middle stage. There is a big step from "legal culture" to actual laws and legal institutions. The assumption in this book is that American society (and others like it) allow the transformation to take place, though how this is done is unpredictable, full of mysterious twists and turns. Despotic societies are not so forthcoming. They keep the cork in the bottle; when the pressure mounts up, the whole society may explode. In the United States, for all its inequalities of wealth, power, and knowledge, the process goes on, however haltingly. Attitudes become processes and processes become institutions.

If my explanations for what has happened make sense, there are some modest lessons to be learned. One lesson is that the trend toward total justice is deep and powerful. Many changes in the legal system seem to have the hard metallic ring of an irresistible process. It would be too strong to say they are "determined" or "inevitable," but they have deep roots in the American past. For that matter, they have deep roots in those massive structural changes that have utterly transformed the whole Western world.

Legalization itself is about as unavoidable as a process can be, if by legalization is meant the proliferation of formal rules, regulations, and procedures. This has to be, simply as a matter of scale. The corner candy store can try to run itself without red tape and formal rules, on a day-by-day basis. JC Penney cannot. It simply *has* to formalize; there is no other way to manage great enterprise.

But it is often a matter of more or less. Two points have to be made about the United States in the 1980s. First, even the corner candy store is enmeshed in rules and regulations. It cannot discriminate against racial minorities, it has to pay sales tax, it is subject to labor laws, and so on. The corner candy store is not an island. For one thing, the store probably does not *make* candy; it buys candy from wholesalers, and sells it. It is part of a marketing and manufacturing chain. Legalization thus engulfs even the tiniest businesses.

Second, there is a distinction between rules that a big company imposes on itself and the rules that come from outside. JC Penney must certainly formalize its empire. It must have rules about accounting, inventory, personnel management, and so on. But there are literally hundreds of rules that come from government. To many people, this distinction between inside and outside is absolutely crucial. Some economists argue that Penney's own rules are bound to be efficient. If not, the company will sink of its own weight. Government rules, on the other hand, will tend to be inefficient; they will hinder the company, and hurt the economy.

This may or may not be so. But "outside" rules do not necessarily add to the degree of legalization. They may merely replace one set of rules with another. There are, after all, two ways of looking at legalization. One way is to adopt a strict definition of law, confining it to official rules and regulations—governmental control. Another is to adopt a loose definition, treating as the "law" of a business or hospital those rules and procedures that would be "law" if imposed by government. Under this second definition, the amount of "law" in society is not determined by official rules only, but rather by *all* rules, public or private. Government rules may be nothing but substitutes for private rules. For example, many companies once had rules or practices that kept black workers down, confining them to dirty, menial work. Government has stepped in and replaced that "rule" with new rules that prohibit such discrimination. Rules against discrimination add to the company's burden; but these rules would not be needed without the prior rules (or practices that amounted to rules) that went the other way. (From the standpoint of rule consumers, black workers for example, a rule is a rule regardless of who promulgates it, so long as it has an impact on them; and regardless of whether it is a "rule" of practice, or an actual, formal rule. They judge rules by their content, not by source or by form.)

I do not claim, of course, that all of the tremendous amount of legalization and formalization in modern life can be accounted for by the substitution of public rules for private ones, or by the development of parallel systems of public and private rules. A vast amount of legalization is the product of the welfare state and the new legal culture— the generalized expectation of justice. These have increased enormously the demands on the legal system. Out of this rich stew of norms comes a fearful amount of fresh law.

That has been the central message of this book. The normative question has been side-stepped. But a reader will inevitably ask: on the whole, is this climate of higher expectations good or bad for society? My answer has to be wishy-washy and probably disappointing. It is that nobody knows. A lot of people think they know. It is clear to them (but not to me) that the legal climate is bad. These people think we live in an incurably litigious society; that we are plagued with procedural complexities, confusions, and delays. They see too much legal process, too much quasi-legal process, too much complaining and fussing by citizens, too much rehashing of issues, too much judicial or administrative review; all this (they feel) clogs the national arteries, holds back important projects, poisons the social atmosphere, and so on. Moreover, there is just too much government, too much regulation, too much taxing and spending. Chapter 1 began with these complaints.

To assess big government and the welfare state is beyond the scope of this book. But I do have a view about the microlevel complaint, about litigation and due process. I have argued that there is no real evidence to back up the most strident complaints. There is not much hope of getting evidence to "prove" the case against litigation and due process. At most, there is evidence that some forms of legalization are inefficient. It costs a lot, in dollars and cents, to impose rules on businesses. This is the price society pays for not letting enterprise do whatever it wants, for curtailing the market, for revamping the classic common law.

But this "inefficiency" is balanced by gains in social justice; not merely in some abstract, philosophical sense, which is important but cannot be measured, but in social justice in the concrete sense of consumer satisfaction. A society moving toward total justice is (one hopes) a society that tries to offer its public many ways to express their grievances, many ways to look for satisfaction of their wrongs. This may not succeed; it may lull people into false consciousness; it may come at too high a price. On the other side, some people argue that this society falls terribly short of the goal of achieving justice; that it does worse than many other, simpler, societies.[1] For one reason or another, then, "total justice" may be a mirage.

The arguments are worth considering. I have tried to tell a complicated story in a few pages. Naturally, a lot gets left out, and a lot gets oversimplified. I have tried to describe prevailing attitudes, past and present; this means generalizing a great deal. I made little or no mention, for example, of the role of economic conflict in American history—the struggle over goods and resources, the drive for money and power, the rivalry that divides rich from poor, group from group. I have also ignored countervailing trends, except when they directly affected the main line of the story. Not everybody accepts the premises of what I have called total justice. Those who do not are not necessarily quiescent and accepting. Every trend produces a countertrend.

The essential arguments here are that certain new principles— sometimes I called them superprinciples—are developing; that these principles make themselves felt in the law, though sometimes not explicitly, and often in a piecemeal way. The reader is entitled to ask: why implicit? why piecemeal? What keeps the principles from sweeping everything before them, if they are so powerful, so deeply rooted in social norms?

The answer is: piecemeal and implicit precisely because of countertrends, opposition, or doubts about each and every application. It is because these principles generate their own discontents, their own dissatisfactions, as they work themselves into practice. Total justice is only a phrase. Justice is never really total; that would be impossible. In many situations, one person's justice is another's injustice. In any event, every generation redefines justice on its own. Justice is always tentative and imperfect, from any point of view.

Still, having said all this, I have to confess my personal sense of pleasure over many of the developments described. I like the spread of due process; I like the welfare state; I like justice for minorities; I like the broader meaning of equality, the great reach and depth of individual rights.

In the abstract, one could indeed argue that this society would be better or less conflicted if there were clear notions about who should be on top, and why; if the average person (who of course is not on top) accepted the stratification system as right and proper; if minorities were grateful for whatever crumbs the majority gave them; if women cooked dinner and darned socks, accepting their place in the family with humble cheer. None of this is possible anymore, for whatever reason. A smashed social order cannot be glued together. And, in any event, social orders do not "smash," except in extreme cases. Instead, they molt and grow a new skin. The old one is a heap of dead cells.

Most people today accept at least parts of the civil rights revolution. Not totally, of course: many whites grumble that the movement went too fast and too far. Many blacks feel it goes too slow. But almost nobody openly defends race relations as they were in the days before *Brown*. The public in general accepts some aspects of legalization and gripes about others. Overall, there is no chance of turning back. There is little chance, either, of reversing any of the major trends in the rest of the law. That nineteenth-century tort law would come back to life is inconceivable. Extinct is forever.

This does not mean, of course, that the movement toward total justice is bound to continue. As I said, every trend promotes or produces a countertrend, and all social movements generate opposition. There is a genuine tax revolt. The ERA was defeated. Proposed ordinances on gay rights are buried by voters saying no. Legislatures try to curb lawsuits against doctors and hospitals. Deregulation is a buzzword of the day. Complaints about law are symptoms of discontent, symptoms of the urge to buck the trends.

If I had to guess, I would probably make this prediction: the new legal culture—the general expectation of justice and its corollaries— may buckle and bend, but it will not go away. It is not an accident, a technical error, a lawyer's trick. It has survival value, and survival power. It is a basic feature of American life, a tribal custom by now, unshakable at the core, deeply germane. It has penetrated into the marrow of people's bones. It is fundamental to modern society, and in essence, for the short run at least, it seems to be here to stay.

NOTES

1. See Laura Nader, ed., *No Access to Law* (1980).

9

EPILOGUE: A NOTE ON THE WIDE, WIDE WORLD

THIS WAS A MONOGRAPH about changes in American law and American legal culture. Examples came from the history of this country and its experience, with only a few exceptions. A reader is bound to ask: are these changes peculiar to the United States, or are they more general? Are these trends going on all over the Western world?

This is not easy to answer. There is not much systematic information on comparative legal culture. There is even less systematic theory to explain what information there is.[1] Legal systems seem to be very different in different countries, although some legal scholars talk hopefully about convergence. There is good reason to believe that the general lines of change run parallel in all the Western, industrial countries. Certainly expanded liability in torts, for example, is a general phenomenon, by no means confined to the United States. It marches on, in both common law and civil law countries.[2]

And, in fact, some changes in law that are symptoms of "total justice" are more pronounced in Europe than in the United States.

Tenant and worker rights are more vested; job security and tenure are more deeply rooted. The welfare state goes further in Europe than in the United States. Historically, the United States was even something of a laggard. Germany and Great Britain adopted workmen's compensation many years before any of the states took this step. Welfare and regulatory law is most definitely international.

What is arguably American is the emphasis on courts, on litigation, on claims-consciousness. This may be peculiar to this country; or perhaps the American version of modern rights-consciousness is peculiarly aggravated. Other countries may be partially or totally immune. Similarly, what I have called plural equality is almost certainly more advanced here than elsewhere; it seems American to the core. I doubt that one could make out as strong a case for plural equality in Norway or Switzerland, or even in neighboring Canada, where, as Edgar Friedenberg has put it, "Foreigners are not rejected . . . but foreignness is; it is something you owe it to yourself to get over."[3] This, however, does not rule out the possibility that there is more plural equality in Canada or Norway or Switzerland than there was in the nineteenth century.

In Part I, I referred to studies of litigation rates. The Toharia study showed that formal litigation was, if anything, declining in Spain. This study, and those that followed it, strongly suggested that the "litigation explosion" was exaggerated, at least as conventionally conceived, and at least in the countries examined. But the Toharia study did not suggest that Spain was immune to legalization. Indeed, Toharia's data on notaries pointed in the opposite direction. The data suggested a general increase in the use of legal mechanisms, even though businessmen and the public avoided formal courts as much as possible. In the United States, too, there is evidence of greater use of alternate forms of dispute settlement and claims procedures, inside and outside of government. There is a real "explosion," for example, of hearings within administrative agencies.[4] This undoubtedly has parallels in Europe.

For what it is worth, too, there are persistent complaints about legal explosions outside the United States. In Germany, for example, one hears complaints about "excess legalization," the "flood of legislation," and so on. Certainly, no two countries and no two legal cultures are alike. But claims-consciousness or something like it is probably on the rise in country after country. There has certainly been a boom in judicial review in the last generation in Germany, Italy, and even Japan. It is superficial to blame it all on American influence.

In fact, it would be odd indeed if the trends described in this book did *not* have parallels in the other parliamentary, welfare states. (The socialist countries, or countries of the third world, are another question.) Some of the factors I pulled out of the dizzying mass of historical fact are quite general: the reduction of insecurity, for example. Modern medicine is the common property of all the Western nations. Legal reactions should have at least a certain functional similarity. Thus, no one should be surprised to find significant differences between, say, the legal cultures and systems of France and Bangladesh; yet, with regard to some areas of law, and some parts of the third world, it would not be a surprise to find considerable "convergence." At the very least, it would be good to have more research.

Each field of law, each area of legal control, is its own rich mix of the particular and the general. In broad outline, the Western nations have shared a single common experience in economic and social development. When we stand far enough above the scene, the trends all begin to look very much the same. The closer down we get, the more differences we see.

For example, the collapse of the Victorian compromise was not just an American phenomenon. It was certainly paralleled in Great Britain, perhaps also in Europe as a whole. The British raised their age of consent in the late nineteenth century; they tightened their laws against sexual deviance. Prohibition, however, was strictly an American madness. And many European countries chose to regulate prostitution rather than banning it.

Perhaps Americans had to ban prostitution, not regulate it, because of an unusually firm commitment to the concept of a single moral code. Perhaps, when this notion crashed, when plural equality replaced it, the changes went broader and deeper than they did in England or Europe. Perhaps the English and Europeans expected less from their lower orders, and hence demanded less. Or, to put it another way, the line between classes and strata was sharper abroad than in this country. Hence a greater need was felt in America to police the moral borders. It is like a country with an enemy just over the frontier. The country will spend more on defense if the border runs through flat and open country than if the boundary line is the ridge of a wind-swept sierra, remote and impassable to troops.

NOTES

1. For an attempt to study legal systems and legal cultures systematically and quantitatively in a comparative vein, see John Merryman, David Clark, and Lawrence M. Friedman, eds., *Law and Social Change in Mediterranean Europe and Latin America* (1979).

2. There are, to be sure, marked differences, some rather important, in the scope of liability; but everywhere there are "unmistakable moves toward stricter liability." Michael Whincup, "Product Liability Laws in Common Market Countries," *Common Market Law Review* 19 (1982):520, 537.

3. Edgar Z. Friedenberg, *Deference to Authority: The Case of Canada* (1980), pp. 154–155. Friedenberg found a striking contrast between Canada and California. To Friedenberg, California has "a genuine and deeply rooted cultural pluralism." Canada, on the other hand, owes a great deal to British culture, which lacks this pluralism, perhaps because, as a "hugely successful colonial power," Great Britain "had reason to maintain and defend its insularity."

4. See, for example, Jerry L. Mashaw, *Bureaucratic Justice: Managing Social Security Disability Claims* (1983).

ACKNOWLEDGMENTS

The generosity of the Russell Sage Foundation made this book possible. I want to thank John Ely, Robert Gordon, Thomas C. Grey, Robert Kagan, John Henry Merryman, Deborah Rhode, William Simon, and Robert Weisberg, for their valuable comments. Douglas Schwartz helped with the research.

INDEX

A

abortion, 46, 98, 128, 135, 142
accidents, 18, 51, 53–56, 60, 66, 68, 71, 100, 109; industrial, 65–66; at work, 49, 55–56, 59, 64, 66, 68, 71; *see also* disability; injury; personal injuries
"acts of God," 89
Adams, John, 70
adultery, 128–129, 131–132, 139
Africans, 117, 119–120
age, 107; of consent, 139, 155; discrimination, 74, 87
Age Discrimination in Employment Act, 87
agencies, 12, 26; administrative, 3, 10–12, 81, 154; government, 119; rules and regulations by, 14
Alabama, 21, 131; Sumpter County suits, 101
alcohol use, 64, 101, 134, 138–140; in traffic, 24; *see also* prohibition; temperance movement
Alger, Horatio, 103
ambulance chasing, 25–26
America, *see* United States
American Nazi Party, 122
Americans, 30, 109, 112–113, 116, 128; claims-conscious, 99–101, 106, 123; native, 115, 120, 130; nineteenth century, 48, 104, 110
Amish, 117–118
antilottery law, 135
antitrust law, 21, 53; *see also* court cases
Arkansas, 138
army, 45–46, 83–85, 121
Asians, 109, 117, 119–120; discrimination against, 73, 82, 112–113, 137
assimilation, 113, 118, 120, 122
Atlantic Reporter, 62
attitudes,97, 108, 119, 121, 148, 151; about law, 31–32, 97–98

"at-will" employment, 74–75
authority, 13, 30, 41, 69, 85, 89–90, 100, 104, 127, 144; administrative, 83; decline of, 89; of teachers, 12–13
autonomy, of legal system, 27–29
awards for damages, 61–62, 66; *see also* compensation; recovery

B

Baldwin, Joseph, 100–101
Bangladesh, 155
bankruptcy, 50, 72–73; law, 72–73
Barbary Coast, 136
Barron v. *Baltimore*, 82
Battle of Verdun, 22
behavior, changes in, 104–106; *see also* legal behavior; sexual behavior
Bible, 128–130
bilingual education, 122
Bill of Rights, 81–82, 86–87, 111, 114; *see also* Constitution of the United States
Black, Donald, 12
Black Muslims, 87
blacks, 98–99, 119, 121–123, 125n38, 140–141, 152; American, 109; discrimination against, 73, 83, 85–86, 89; rights of, 111–112; Southern, 111, 141
blasphemy, 113, 115–116, 131; law, 114–115
Bletter v. *Harcourt, Brace & World, Inc.*, 66–67
Board of Education, 90
Bob Jones University, 119
Bok, Derek, 7, 10
Boston, 130–132, 135
Brown, Edmund G., Jr., 90
Brownsville affair, 83–85, 88–89
Brown v. *Board of Education*, 87, 152
Brown v. *Kendall*, 54–55
Buddha, 114

Buddhists, 113
budget: of Massachusetts, 31; of the U.S. government, 45–46
Burger, Chief Justice, 117
Burroughs, Christopher, 129
business, 54, 63, 149; concerns, 12, 21

C

calamities, see disasters
California, 12, 18–19, 67, 87, 89, 103–105, 137–139, 156n3; Alameda County studies, 17, 82, 139; court cases, 61, 89; laws, 137; Penal Code, 137
California Constitutional Convention, 113
Canada, 154, 156n3
case law, 63, 81, 119, 143
cases, see court cases
Castro, Fidel, 122
Catholics, 84, 140
Census Bureau, 17
Chandler, Thomas Jefferson, 114
change: in concept of equality, 110; legal, 30,32, 38, 80, 97, 100, 102, 104, 119–120, 123, 131, 140, 147–148, 153; social, 18, 30–32, 34, 38, 59, 80, 89, 107, 147
Chicago, 47, 89, 109, 132–133, 136
children, 47–48, 50, 52, 87, 99, 103–104; education of, 39–40; and school, 12, 45, 84, 86, 118, 122–123
China, 83; People's Republic of, 107; see also Asians
Christian, Joseph, 86
Christianity, 112–116; see also Catholics; Protestants
church, 86, 102, 113–114, 116, 129, 131, 133, 145n5
Cincinnati, 139
civil rights: cases, 21; law, 120; movement, 87, 115, 141; revolution, 152
Civil Rights Acts, 21, 73, 87
claims, 18, 26, 61, 89, 97, 100, 106, 154; agents, 26; explosion, 100
claims-consciousness, 76, 97–101, 106, 123, 154–155; in the United States, 100
codes: criminal, 128; dress, 12–13, 119; social, 118; see also moral code
cohabitation, 104, 143
collective action, 68, 70
colonial period, 8, 101, 127, 129–130; "blue laws," 127; law, 128–129, 130
colonies, 19, 33, 113
common law, 9, 11, 53, 113, 150, 153; age, 139; courts, 101; systems, 20
compensation, 49, 51, 59–68, 144; theory of,

60–63; total, 63; see also recompense; recovery for losses; workmen's compensation
complaints: against lawyers, 10, 16; against the role of law in modern society, 150–152, 154
Comstock law, 135
conflict, 25, 118, 123; economic, 151; social, 109
conformity, 102–104
Congress, 3, 47, 72, 83, 85, 87, 116, 135, 137–1138
Connecticut law, 142
Constitutions: state and federal, 82; of the United states, 72, 80–81, 115–116
contract: law, 31, 76, 78n30; right, 75; see also employment contracts
control, 40–42, 44n4, 51, 141–142; governmental, 12, 69, 149; legal, 155; social, 133; of wages and prices, 70
corporations, 10, 23; private, 10
court cases, 4, 18–23, 55–62, 82–91, 101, 108, 112, 114–118, 129, 132, 137, 142–143; antitrust, 21–22; appellate, 60; civil, 82; civil rights, 21; commercial, 78n30; criminal, 81–82, 111; disciplinary, 88; due process, 80; federal, 13; immigration, 82–83; malpractice, 89–91; nineteenth century, 59; polygamy, 116; of products liability, 59, 61; railroad, 55–59; school, 13; tort, 57, 61; see also lawsuits
courts, 3, 5, 11, 15–20, 22, 26–29, 36n34, 36n38, 39, 57–59, 61–66, 74–76, 78n30, 85–87, 100, 118–119, 127, 129–132; American, 82; appeal, 62; colonial, 101; common-law, 101; federal, 16, 82–83, 87; formal, 154; local, 16; nineteenth century, 54, 58; Spanish, 18; state, 16–18, 82
crime, 52, 67, 82, 86, 103, 128–131, 135, 143; against morality, 137–139; see also sin; torts; vice
criminals, rights of, 82, 89
crisis, 4, 27, 30, 90, 140; of integration and social stability, 7; in the legal system, 6–7, 26, 29; legitimation, 27, 29–30; oil, 34
Crow, Jim, 141
culture, 98, 108, 119–120, 122–123; majority, 140; see also legal culture; political culture

D

Dalai Lama, 115
damage recoveries, 22, 53–55, 61–63; see also awards for damages
Darwin, Charles, 123

death, 48–52
debauchery, 135, 137–138, 142
Defense Department, 31
definition: of law, 29, 41
Delaware: court cases, 114, 129
delegalization, 126–127
demands, 5, 27, 31–32, 69, 71, 106, 148; on
  government, 51; and responses, 33–34, 42,
  46–47, 105, 107
Denmark, 34
Department of Motor Vehicles, 89
dependence, social, 104–106
de Tocqueville, Alexis, 112
Detroit, 132
Dictionary of Americanisms, 25
disability, 64–65, 107
disasters, 43, 48–51, 57–59, 65, 71–72, 144;
  economic, 49
discrimination, 21, 73–74, 87, 108, 149; *see
  also specific issues*
diseases, 48–49, 51, 70–71, 79n58, 137
disputes, 18–19, 23, 88, 154
divorce, 19, 22, 52, 127; law, 126; no-fault,
  26, 126
doctors, 90–91, 152
doctrine, 11, 13, 54–56, 58–61, 72; of
  courts, 116; of immutability, 110; of retaliatory eviction, 73–74
drugs, 46–47, 137–140; addition to, 128,
  137, 139
due process, 24, 70, 76, 80–85, 88, 92n13,
  93n32, 106, 150–151; explosion, 91; procedural, 88; revolution, 76, 80–81, 87, 89,
  99, 143, 147

E

Ecclesiastes, 11
economy, 33–34, 40, 49–50, 68, 70, 149;
  development of, 155; expansion of, 18;
  growth of, 53, 56; needs, 55; security of, 65
education, 13, 39–40, 117–118, 121–123,
  134, 144; bilingual, 13; *see also* school
Edwards v. *Habib*, 73
Eighteenth Amendment, 138
eighteenth century, 69, 72, 129, 131–132
elderly, 71, 99; rights of, 120
employees, 12, 16, 55, 64, 66, 69; *see also*
  workers
employers, 49, 55, 67, 74–75, 85, 119; rights
  of, 85
employment: contracts, 74–75; law, 75; *see
  also* "at-will" employment; jobs
England, 33, 48, 81, 131, 139, 155
equality, 97, 101, 107, 110–112, 115, 119–

121, 123, 140–141; concept of, 97, 107,
  110, 151; legal, 111; movement for racial,
  87; redefinition of, 120; *see also* plural
  equality
equal rights, 110, 112, 141; protection, 80
ERA, 152; *see also* feminist movement; wom-
  en
estrangement, in social relations, 90–91
ethnicity, 107, 109–110, 113; *see also* race;
  religion; *specific ethnic groups*
Europe, 7, 32, 34, 112, 116–117, 136, 140,
  153–155; absolutist states of, 40; medieval,
  38; *see also individual countries*
evolution, 123
expectations, 27, 34, 46, 52, 63, 78n30, 100,
  106–107, 150; private and social, 76; reciprocal, 106; *see also* general expectations of
  justice; general expectations of recompense

F

fairness, 24, 43, 51, 72, 75, 81, 88, 91, 101
family, 39, 43, 52, 73, 121, 133; law, 31, 76,
  126; life, 75, 102
Farwell v. *Boston and Worcester Rr.*, 55–56
fault, principle of, 54, 58–59, 64, 68
FBI, 46
Federal Register, 12
fellow-servant rule, 55–57, 59, 64, 68; *see
  also* workmen's compensation
feminist movement, 87
Fifth Amendment, 80–82
First Amendment, 118–119
Food and Drug Administration (FDA), 47
food and drugs: law, 42, 46–47; regulation of,
  47
Ford Motor Company, 61
foreigners, 120, 122, 154; *see also* immigrants
formalization, 148–150
formal law, 91, 133
fornication, 103, 128–131, 139, 143, 145,
  145n5
Fourteenth Amendment, 80, 82
France, 9, 14, 73, 99, 155
freedom, 24, 104, 112; of choice, 143; of mobility, 24; personal, 24; of religion, 114,
  116–119, 129; of speech, 85, 118
French, Thomas, 129
Friedenberg, Edgar, 154
Frontiero v. *Richardson*, 108

G

Garza, Emilia, 132
gays, 140, 143; rights of, 84, 152

general expectation of justice, 5, 43, 51, 72–
    73, 75–76, 88, 97–98, 120–121, 123,
    144, 150, 152
general expectation of recompense, 5, 43, 52,
    60, 75–76, 144
General Motors, 12, 106
Georgia, 139; Supreme Court, 112
Germany, 154–155
The Gilded Age (Mark Twain/Dudley War-
    ner), 49
government, 10, 13, 16, 23, 31–32, 41–43,
    46, 68–70, 81–82, 85, 89, 101, 121, 144,
    149–150, 154; American, 31, 45, 69; ex-
    pansion of, 70; federal, 21, 31, 45, 87;
    nineteenth century, 68–69; payments, 45–
    46; Western, 5–6
Great Britain, 9, 154–155, 156n3; *see also*
    England
grievance procedures, 74, 88
growth: economic, 53, 56; of the legal profes-
    sion, 8; of legislation, 11–12; of popula-
    tion, 31, 34
Gusfield, Joseph, 140

H

Habermas, Juergen, 29
Hammurabi, 53
handicapped, 85, 92n22, 121, 140; rights of,
    13, 84, 88
Harrison Act, 137–138
Hartog, Hendrik, 69
Hasson, James, 61
health, 48, 136–137; 140–141; public, 70,
    79n58, 139; *see also* diseases; food and
    drugs; medicine
Hindus, Michael S., 103
Hispanics, 121; Mexican-Americans, 21,
    137; Puerto Ricans, 115
Hobbes, 47
Holland, 9, 34
Holy Scriptures, 115
Honolulu, 136
hospitals, 12, 21, 83, 90, 149, 152; VA (Vet-
    eran's Administration), 45
Hurst Willard, 56
Hyde, Alan, 30
"hyperlexis," 16, 20; *see also* litigation

I

IBM, 21
Idaho statute, 64–65
ideology, 28, 69; changes in, 104

Illinois: court case (Cook County), 89; drug
    law, 137
immigrants, 105, 140; in the United States,
    120, 140
immigration, 83, 130; law, 83
immorality, 60, 135, 137, 139
immunity from law, 22, 42, 83–85, 87, 120,
    126, 154
immutability, biological and social, 107–110
independence, structural, 28–29; *see also* au-
    tonomy
India, 104
Indiana, 131
individualism, 39–40, 101–107, 121–123
Industrial Revolution, 32, 42, 52–53
injury, 25, 54–55, 57, 60–64, 66, 68, 100;
    see also accidents; personal injuries
injustice, 50, 71, 89, 110, 151
institutions: legal, 4, 25, 30, 148; public and
    private, 12, 81, 83, 85, 88–89, 144, 147
insurance, 16, 25, 58–60, 63, 67, 72, 90;
    companies, 18, 25–26; expansion of, 59;
    life, 49; social, 48, 67–68, 76; unemploy-
    ment, 48, 71; in the United States, 49
interdependence of modern society, 105–106
Irish-Americans, 99
Islam, 114
Italy, 9, 18, 155

J

Jackson, J., 118
Japan, 9, 155
JC Penney, 148–149
Jefferson, Thomas, 31, 70
Jehovah's Witnesses, 118, 140
Jesus Christ, 113–115
Jews, 113, 140
jobs: loss of, 52, 71, 105; political, 10; protec-
    tion of, 74; security of, 65, 154; for
    women, 121
Johnson administration, 21
judges, 3, 16, 18–19, 26, 39, 56, 58, 61–62,
    75–76, 115, 119–120
The Jungle (Upton Sinclair), 47
jurors, 62–63
jury, 18, 61–63
justice, 5, 16, 23, 30, 43, 50–51, 70, 91, 99,
    101, 112, 144, 151; civilian, 85; cosmic,
    50; military, 83–85; perfect, 20; social, 51,
    150; total, 5, 31, 63, 67, 70, 91, 106, 110,
    126, 144–145, 147–148, 150–153; *see also*
    general expectation of justice

K

Kinsey Report, 142
knowledge, as power, 70
Ku Klux Klan, 122

L

labor law, 74, 85, 147, 149
laissez faire, 69–70, 126
landlord and tenant, 73–74, 106–107, 154; law of, 52, 73–74, 147
language, as issue in America, 115, 122
law: in American society, 3, 5, 25, 148; change in, 104; change through, 31, 42; constitutional, 147; dependence on society, 26–28; enforcement, 133–134, 138; excess, 7, 11–15; scope of, 42; size of, 19, 23; in traditional societies, 39; *see also specific laws*
law explosion, 3–7, 20, 32, 127
Laws and Liberties of Massachusetts, 128–129
lawsuits, 8, 21–22, 101, 132, 152; *see also* litigation
lawyers, 3–5, 16, 22–26, 29, 88, 90, 119–120; demand for, 10; excess, 7–10, 14, 23, 25; and law of torts, 52–53, 59; litigation, 19; nineteenth century, 101, 112
legal act, 13–15, 33
legal behavior, 13–15, 20, 29, 31, 60, 99, 103, 123
legal character, 99, 102, 144, 147; American, 97, 99, 123
legal culture, 5, 30–34, 44n4, 51, 57, 61, 63, 69, 72–73, 81, 91, 107–108, 116–120, 123, 131, 143–144, 147–148, 150, 152–155; American, 38–43, 76, 97, 107, 126; changes in, 32, 52, 97–100, 143; comparative, 153; modern, 75, 88, 107, 144; nineteenth century, 120
legalization, 12, 148–150, 152, 154
legal process, 3–5, 19, 42, 150
legal system, 13, 22–31, 33, 51, 97, 147–148, 153; American, 6–8, 23, 72, 127; changes in, 4–5, 30, 148; crisis in, 6–7, 26, 29; demands on, 81, 150; measurement of, 11, 14–17, 19; modern, 7, 20; of the nineteenth century, 69, 112; of Western governments, 6
legal theory, 60, 62, 74; American, 69
legislation, *see* statutes
legislatures, 10, 26, 66, 82, 85, 140, 143, 152; state, 3

legitimacy, 6, 29–30, 134, 140–141, 143–144
legitimation crisis, 7, 30
liability, 54, 56–60, 62–63, 153, 156n2; general expectation of, 49
Lieberman, Jethro K., 16, 60
life, conditions of: in contemporary society, 7, 40, 105; in nineteenth century, 47–52
Lincoln, Abraham, 31
Lippmann, Walter, 136
litigation, 5, 6, 7, 10, 14–23, 25, 35n21, 54, 64, 76, 82, 90–91, 98, 101, 150; federal, 16; rates, 17, 19–20, 100, 154; in the United States, 14, 17–19; *see also* court cases; lawsuits; lawyers
litigation explosion, 5–6, 15–20, 35n18, 154
"living law," 29, 103, 108, 111, 116, 134
London, criminal courts of, 131
Louie v. Bamboo Gardens, 65–68
Luhmann, Niklas, 28
Lumpkin, Joseph H., 112
Lynch v. Donnelly, 125n28

M

machines, 42, 51, 53, 65
Maine, 115
malpractice, 21, 76, 89–91, 145, 152; explosion, 90–91
Mann Act, 135
Married Women's Property Laws, 111
Marvin v. Marvin, 75, 143
Maryland: court case, 115; law, 113
Massachusetts, 8, 31; Bay colony, 8; colonial, 113, 128–130; Puritan, 39
McGuffey's Readers, 121–122
measurement, of size of legal system, 11, 14–17, 19
medicine, 70–71, 90, 105, 155; age of modern, 42; in the nineteenth century, 47; *see also* diseases; doctors; health
megacases, 21–22
mental patients, rights of, 87, 89
"meter-running," 10
Michael M. v. Superior Court, 146n38
Michigan: law, 136
Miller, Wallace, 117
minorities, 119–120, 123, 140–141, 151–152; linguistic, 115; racial, 24, 89, 149; rights of, 84, 119; *see also specific groups*
Mississippi, 64, 101, 139
Mohammed, 114–115
moral code, 118, 122, 131, 135, 141, 143, 155

moral hegemony, 119, 134, 141
morality: morals, 75, 102–104, 115, 127,
    131, 133–134, 138–139, 141–142; Bibli-
    cal, 123; sexual, 103, 107, 142; traditional,
    127
moral offenses, 128, 131, 134, 138
Mormons, 99, 112, 116–117
Moslems, 113

N

Nader, Laura, 23–24
narcotics, see drugs
National Guard, 46
National Labor Relations Board, 85
Natus, Frank, 83
Nazi Germany, 82
Nebraska, 115
negligence, 55, 57, 59, 64, 68, 74; compara-
    tive, 64; contributory, 54, 63–64
Nelson, William, 130
Nevada, 146n24
New Deal, 45
New England, 129; states, 62
New Hampshire, Bill of Rights of, 114
New Jersey, 74
New Orleans, 132, 136
New York, 64, 130, 132, 136, 139; court
    case, 114
nineteenth century, 11–13, 17, 19–20, 42,
    47–53, 61–63, 68–70, 81–82, 84–86,
    101–106, 111–114, 118, 120–121, 131–
    134, 154–155; see also specific issues
nonconformity, 39, 102, 143, 143–144; see
    also individualism
norms, 7, 12, 32, 41, 60, 72, 97–99, 103,
    112, 127, 140, 144, 150; official, 133–
    134, 142; sexual, 141; social, 74–75, 110,
    147, 151; of total justice, 67
North Dakota, 13
Norway, 154

O

O'Connell, Jeffrey, 100
Ohio, Revised Statutes of, 11
Old Order Amish, 118
opinions: about law, 31–32, 98–99, 111;
    public, 39, 47, 130; see also legal culture
Oregon, 103, 105

P

Pacific Reporter, 62
Pennsylvania: court cases, 84, 86

People v. Ruggles, 114
personal injuries, 18, 25, 53–54, 61–62; law
    of, 52, 154; recovery for, 61–62; see also
    accidents; compensation; damage re-
    coveries; general expectation of recompense
pioneers, 100, 102–105; see also immigrants
plural equality, 107–108, 113, 115, 119–
    122, 141–143, 154–155
pluralism, 119–120, 122
police, 3, 13, 29, 46, 103, 131–133, 136,
    138; brutality, 82
political culture, 69, 98, 107; changes in, 81
polygamy, 112, 116–117, 119
poor laws, 48
Pound, Roscoe, 56
prejudice, 83, 111, 119; see also dis-
    crimination
Priestley v. Fowler, 55
Princeton University, 21
prisoners, 45; rights of, 83–87, 120
private law, 13, 52, 76; interaction with
    public law, 31, 72, 91, 150
product safety, 46–47
prohibition, 138, 140, 155
property offenses, 130–131
prostitution, 131–136, 139–140, 144,
    146n24, 155; in the United States, 132
Protestants, 102, 111–113, 140
public law, 13, 52; interaction with private
    law, 31, 72, 91, 150
Pure Food and Drug Act, 47
Puritans, 39, 127–129

R

Rabin, Robert L., 54, 57
race, 107–113, 116, 134, 141–142, 144,
    152; discrimination, 21, 74, 87, 119; dis-
    crimination law, 87; statutory definition,
    109; see also Asians; blacks; whites
racism, 82–83, 119
railroads, 53, 55–57, 69
rape, 97, 127, 139; statutory, 139
Reagan administration, 22
Reagan, Ronald, 116
recompense, see general expectation of re-
    compense
recovery for losses, 54–55, 57, 59–64, 67; see
    also damage recoveries
regulations, 3–4, 12–14, 24, 29, 40, 42, 47,
    144–145, 147–149; of food, 47; see also
    rules
Reid, John Philip, 103
Reid, Oscar W., 83

religion, 50, 52, 74, 86, 107, 110, 112–119, 122, 128–129, 134, 144; discrimination, 74; minority, 116–117; traditional, 118; in the United States, 113, 116, 128; *see also* church; God; *specific religions and sects*
repression, sexual, 141–142
responses, *see* demands
retarded, rights of, 84, 120
Revolution, 8, 114
Reynolds v. *United States*, 116–119
rights, 81, 83–84, 88, 141; American, 140; constitutional, 82; individual, 151; of landlords, 73–74; modern, 120; of privacy, 126; procedural, 80–81; public, 69; tenant and worker, 154; *see also* civil rights; equal rights; *specific groups*
rights-consciousness, 83, 87, 99–101, 154
risk, 55, 58, 66, 105; assumption of, 54–55, 59; spreading of, 58, 71–72
Roe v. *Wade*, 142
Roosevelt, Theodore, 31, 83, 85, 115
Ruffin, Edmund, 50
rules, 3–4, 11–15, 24, 29, 42, 53–57, 68, 127, 144–145, 148–150; of limitation, 55; no-liability, 57; private, 12; *see also* fellow-servant rule
Rules Governing the Regulation of Vice, 133
Ryan v. *New York Central Railroad Co.*, 57–59

S

safety on the job, 12, 65
St. Louis, 17, 132, 136
San Francisco, 83, 112, 136
Saudi Arabia, 9
Scandinavia, 18
school: dress codes, 12–13; dress codes, "legalization" of, 21, 83–85; and opportunity structure, 73; prayer, 116; rules of, 121; theory of education, 117–118, 133; *see also* education; students
science, 41–42, 51, 71, 134, 139, 141–142; age of, 70
Scopes trial, 123
Sears, Roebuck and Company, 39, 100
Securities and Exchange Commission, 49
security, personal desire for, 70, 104–105; *see also* welfare state
self-control, 103, 133–134, 140
seventeenth century, 19, 129–130
sex discrimination, 13, 21, 74, 87, 107–108, 110, 115; laws against, 87
sexual behavior, 97, 103, 126–145, 155; legal

regulation of, 126–128; *see also* sexual offenses
sexual offenses, 128–131; *see also specific issues*
Shaw, Lemuel, 55–57
Simon, Rita J., 100
sin, 129, 131, 139
sixteenth century, 47–48
slavery, 104–105, 109, 111–112; "white," 135
Smith, Adam, 69
Smith, Daniel N., 103
Smith, Rodney, 136
Social Evil in Chicago, 136
social forces, 28–29
social order, 25, 29, 33, 51–52, 152
social "safety net," 105–106, 143; *see also* security
Social Security, 81, 123; Administration, 91
society: automotive, 24; changes in, 97–98; feudal, 52; health of, 137, 140; and individualism, 103–104; "integration" of, 30; litigious, 150; modern, 30, 38–41, 105–106, 144, 152; nineteenth century, 105; no-risk, 71; primitive, 52; relationship to legal system, 24–28; socialist, 107; structure of, 15, 27; traditional, 32, 38–41
sodomy, 128–129, 139
Somes, Mary, 129
Soviet Union, 107
Spain, 18, 20, 154
Stanford University, 88
state: absolutist, 41; intervention of, 31, 34, 106; liberal, 40; modern, 7, 29, 31, 41, 45–46; nineteenth century, 68; power and scope of, 42, 44n 4, 46, 68–71; totalitarian, 28
states, laws of: on fair housing, 73; on insolvency, 50; *see also* statutes
State v. *Chandler*, 114
State v. *West*, 115
statutes: antiabortion, 135; increase in numbers, 11–12; scope of, 46–47
Stone, Lawrence, 47
Story, Joseph, 113
Storyville, 136
students, 16, 73, 88, 122; rights of, 12–13, 83–84, 87–89
superprinciples, 43, 75–76, 81, 88, 144, 151
supply and demand, 9–10, 15, 25
Supreme Court, 28, 80, 82–83, 85, 87, 108–109, 112, 115–118, 125n28, 132, 135, 142
Switzerland, 154

T

Talmud, 53
taxation, 16, 34, 53, 72, 119, 149–150, 152
technology, 32, 42, 51, 71; *see also* science
temperance movement, 138
Tennessee: court case, 137
tenure, 75, 154; principle of, 73–74
Teubner, Gunther, 28
Texas: court cases, 83, 132
Thailand, 99
Third World, 155
Tinker v. *Des Moines*, 84–85, 87
Toharia, José Juan, 18, 20, 154
torts, 52–54, 61, 64, 75, 123, 153; law of, 26, 31, 52–54, 57, 59–60, 63, 65, 67–68, 72, 76, 91, 147; nineteenth century, 57, 59, 152
traditional society, 32, 39; role of law in, 39
traditions: ethnic, 122; legal, 53, 56; Puritan, 127–128; religious, 128
trials, *see* court cases
twentieth century, 17, 59–63, 70, 112, 120, 133, 135, 141

U

uncertainty: factor of, 58; reduction of, 51–52, 59, 71, 100–101, 104, 143
United States, 3, 4, 8, 14–15, 26, 32–34, 107, 112–113, 130, 141, 143, 148–149, 153–155; colonial, 127
University of Denver, 21
U.S. v. *Ju Toy*, 82–83, 88
U.S. v. *Nixon*, 28
Utah, 116

V

values, *see* legal culture
Vermont: court case, 84
Veteran's Administration, 100
vice, 130–131, 133–140; *see also* alcohol use; drugs
victim compensation, *see* compensation

victimless crime, 117, 127–129, 135, 143
"Victorian compromise," 132–135, 139, 144, 155
Vidal v. *Girard Exrs.*, 124n23
Vietnam War, 84
Virginia, 46; Accomack County study, 101; court case, 86; statute book, 46

W

Warren Court, 81
Washington, D.C., 46, 139
Washington, George, 70
WASPs, 140–141
Watch and Ward Society, 135
Webb v. *U.S.*, 137–138
welfare, 34, 48, 67, 72, 154; law, 154; systems, 34
welfare state, 27, 32, 34, 52, 67–68, 71, 76, 101, 105, 150–151, 154–155
Western countries, 4, 33, 62, 71, 105, 107, 116, 153, 155; *see also specific countries*
Western world, 7, 68, 148, 153
White, Edward, 59–60
White, James, 129
White House, 30
whites, 109, 111, 112, 123, 142, 152
Willis, Dorsey, 85
Wisconsin, 64; Chippewa County Study, 17; court case, 117
Wisconsin v. *Yoder*, 117–119
women, 48, 99, 104, 121–122, 140, 152; equality of, 123; rights of, 84, 111, 120
workers, 41, 49, 55–56, 64–65, 74, 85, 87–88, 104, 106; black, 149; factory, 50; nineteenth century, 49
workmen's compensation, 49, 59–60, 63–68, 154
World War I, 111, 136
Wyatt v. *Stickney*, 21

Y

Yick Wo v. *Hopkins*, 112
Yoder, Jonas, 117
Yutzy, Adin, 117